Revelation 12:11

And they defeated him because of the blood of the lamb and because of their testimony...

SOME OF THE NAMES AND CHARACTERS IN THIS BOOK, HAVE BEEN CHANGED TO PROTECT THE INNOCENT!

This book is dedicated to my family and friends everywhere who have prayed and helped me, by being honest enough to say what was really on their hearts. To my husband who is my best friend! He shared what he liked, as well as what he didn't like and I thank him for that honesty. To our daughter who does open-heart surgery with every letter she gives me, making me cry as well as laugh. To our son, Franklin, who has made me a very proud mom. To Kathryn, for your encouragement and prayers and the time you spent bringing this baby forth! And thanks to Hal and Kelley, who prayed us through many a storm; to my sweet mama who has always been there for me; and to Randy, a special friend who made this book cover come alive. I thank God I have the most wonderful family and friends in the world and I want them all to know this, **just one more time!!! To a man I have never met, whom God used to bring this boat safely back on course, my thanks to Mr. Kenneth Scott!** And to God, who gave me the words, thoughts, and ideas to bring it all about. You said it would be a supernatural work, Lord, and it was!

A special thank you to Julie Price for taking the time to read and share her thoughts; her feedback helped me to share almost more than I wanted to in this book. A special thanks to two very special women: Robbie Poole and Patricia Thompson; they were the seed planters of "you really need to write a book!" Their encouragement is part of the reason this book is in print.

In John 14:15, Jesus said, 'If you love me, you're going to obey these things that I've shown you to do'! One of those things was writing this book. I had to pray about loving God. Pray about it? Pray to fall in love with God? Yes! God gave a message to the church in Ephesus and He had one for me, too. Revelation 2:3-4 said 'you have patiently suffered for me without quitting. Yes, I was tireless in my work efforts in the church throughout the years but I have this against you, Wanda Reuben. You don't love me as you did at first.' God, I want to be in love with You; I want to love You with all my heart. I prayed for this to happen many times. Once I fell, I fell hard and then I began to want what God wanted for me more than what I had wanted for myself. "Show me, Lord, who You are" and "Show me, Lord, what You are calling me to do with my life." His reply: "Love me, Wanda, and love others; these are what I require of you".

Table of Contents

The Fairy Tale Begins.   4

I Love To Tell the Story   7

Storms of Fear   9

Great Gusts of Pride   24

A Jealous Wind Blows   35

A Bitter Gale of Unforgiveness   46

A Healing Breeze   61

The Marriage-Go-Round   71

Children – Kids Court   88

Powerful Currents of Prayer   112

**All scripture notations are from the Life Application Bible, New Living Translation

The Fairy Tale Begins

Once upon a time, there lived a princess named Wanda with two precious children, Rebecca and Franklin. There was also a handsome prince named Arnold that lived in the land nearby. When the prince met the princess, they dated and danced the nights away. Many of the princess' subjects and ladies in waiting warned her that this prince was not interested in settling down, but the princess totally ignored their council and decided that this prince was for her! So, with much persuasive talking, the prince was convinced that he could not live without the princess. "The shoe fit!" so they married and lived happily ever after. Now, would you like to hear the real story?

The real story started just like the fairy tale above: The princess with two lovely children met, fell in love, and then married the prince. However, here's where real life and fantasy differed; after they married, they started to live very unhappily. The princess had been wild in her younger days and when she got "saved", she got SAVED. Instead of living in the grace and love of her Savior, she put herself under the law and then proceeded to put everyone else there, too. She felt that if she prayed enough, talked enough, did enough good things, and didn't do the bad things anymore, then everything would be OK! Her good works would surely get a stamp of approval from God. Acting on that premise, the princess became very busy in trying to convince (convict) her family to become Christians. She went from meeting after meeting, trying to get the family to come with her. When they did, they were miserable! Soon the princess became very frustrated with her family and began to lose her joy. She eventually realized that she had been doing nothing but turning her family away from God, playing right into the hands of the enemy (that old fire-breathing dragon!). After traveling down this road for many years, the princess finally learned that love was the way to the heart of people, not the law. If she was going to introduce them to Jesus, they were going to have to see Him in her, right there in their home. The princess also realized that ministry to others was not to be put before her family; being a witness to them was the priority. Oh! How the princess had been deceived! As much as the princess tried to change those she loved (for their own good, of course!), she finally learned that the Holy Spirit was the only one who could bring lasting change and lasting peace in a person.

Fasten Your Seat Belts; It's Full Speed Ahead!

To set the record straight, God gave Princess Wanda a wonderful example to illustrate His point. One day she was making some copies of a news article. As she was putting the paper into the printer, the cardstock went in side-ways. She immediately cut the printer off, figuring she'd be throwing that one away for sure because IT WASN'T PERFECT. But as she looked at it, only a tiny place on the corner was bent and the thought came that it could be used after all. "Why throw away a good piece of cardstock just because it had a small flaw?" she reasoned. The princess began to see that she didn't have to be flawless to be used by God. He didn't need a person with a college degree, someone with all the answers, or a perfect person to accomplish His will. "Just a willing heart and a humble spirit is what God uses to open all sorts of doors" would be the thought that came to her mind. God wanted her to get to know Him and to be led by the Holy Spirit. This would take some time; first, Princess Wanda had to get rid of her religious spirit! Yes, getting to know Him, getting to know all about Him, was the key to this freedom and the most important thing that she could do for herself and her family.

How did the princess deepen her relationship with God? She began by diving into His Word. God said in His Word that the clouds displayed His glory. And that day and night they KEPT ON TELLING ABOUT GOD! (Psalms 19: 1-2) The princess would get to know the Lord by noticing the clouds above and studying his creation. Another thing she learned was that when the Word says to go into your prayer closet and talk with God that the closet could be the bathroom, bedroom, beach, literally anywhere. Yes, she could even talk to Him and hear from Him while riding in her royal coach – a Ford Taurus.

A destructive wind had been blowing in this land of Make-Believe for quite some time. This old, fire-breathing dragon (Satan) wanted the princess and her family destroyed! (John 10:10) But the Lord wanted them to live so He sent a fresh wind to their land. It was the wind of the Holy Spirit. One morning the word came to the princess to look at Ezekiel 37:9. The Lord spoke to her and told her to speak this word over her marriage and her family. And so the princess began to speak "Prophesy unto the wind, prophesy and say to the wind, 'thus saith the Lord. Come from the four winds O breath, and breathe upon these slain that they may live'". The Lord was telling the princess that where the enemy had tried to destroy, the Holy Spirit would restore! The wind of the Holy Spirit would blow away the destruction and the lies of the enemy; the wind of the Holy Spirit would blow away the smoky darkness of despair so that God's light could fill their land. A crop of new fruit (love, peace, joy, etc.) would be planted according to God's plan that would give forth an indestructible harvest. The prince and the princess could live happily ever after, not in the land of Make-Believe but in God's Promised Land! And now it's time to reveal the secret; I'm that princess and my husband, Arnold, is my prince!

I LOVE TO TELL THE STORY

A New Beginning

For many people being born again may sound strange. But I want to share what asking Jesus into my heart has done for me. The new birth I received when I asked Jesus to be Lord of my life gave me a new beginning, a second birth. It gave me a chance to have a face-lift on the inside, so to speak. By becoming a child of the King, I have the opportunity for a new attitude, new desires, new ways to see things and new beginnings every day. It's His gift; all I have to do is <u>choose</u> it.

Quite a few years ago Arnold and I were about to get a divorce and I was a mess. I realized that something wasn't right and I needed help. I had heard about God, knew He existed, and had even been baptized. But I had never been born again. I had never experienced a personal, one-on-one relationship with Jesus as I had with my spouse or a friend. In that moment of marital turmoil, I asked Jesus if He would come into my heart and take over my life. I repented of my sins, although at the time I didn't think there were that many of them. I just knew that I had made many mistakes and the way my life was going just wasn't working out. I released my will that night and asked Jesus for His will to be done in me. I asked Him to show me what He wanted me to do. Soon after this simple prayer, I felt God prompt me to ask Arnold to try making a go of this marriage again with both of us making an effort. Arnold agreed and a new journey began. God's thoughts and ways of doing things turned out so much better than my ways.

What I didn't realize until much later on was that the Holy Spirit had taken hold of my heart. He had been drawing me and convicting me that I <u>needed</u> Jesus as my personal Savior and I <u>needed</u> to repent. John 16:8-9 told me all about the Holy Spirit's work and what He had been doing in my life, without my even knowing it at the time. 'And when He, the Holy Spirit, comes He will convince the world of its sin and of God's righteousness and of the coming judgment.' The world's sin is unbelief in Jesus. That was it in a nutshell. I hadn't believed that I needed to repent; I hadn't believed in a coming judgment; and I hadn't believed that Jesus was the only way for eternal life with God in heaven. Up to that point in time, I thought if I were good enough I'd make it into heaven one day. This was my prayer for a new beginning:

"Father, I do believe Your Word that says Jesus died on the cross for my sins. I know my performance won't get me into heaven or keep me out of there. I want to focus on Jesus and what He did for me on the cross. I repent of all my known sins and the ones I'm not even aware of yet. Jesus, You are the one that saves me. I thank You for all that You did for me that day on the cross. It is Your shed blood that makes me right with God. I ask You to come into my heart and take over every area of my life. I ask You, Holy Spirit, to help me live a life that is pleasing to God and I ask You to release Your power and gifts inside of me so that God may use me until Jesus returns. I pray that You will bring to my mind Your thoughts on the decisions that I need to make. I pray to be as bold as a lion and full of the fear of the Lord. Help me, Lord, to hate what You hate and to love what You love. Give me a new heart, one that is pure and whole and loves others just like You do. Amen."

This prayer was just a beginning for me. My life began to change with each breath as God sent fresh wind my way. The enemy has sure put up a good fight by blowing in a few disturbances. There was quite an unstable air mass for a while. But while the winds may clash and storms brew, the wind from the Holy Spirit overcomes them all. The following chapters are just a few pictures from my life's photo album. My prayer is for the wind of the Holy Spirit to blow in your life so that all destructive forces are struck down and for God's glory through deliverance and fresh anointing be evident!

STORMS OF FEAR

I Had a Grip or Did It Have Me?

I got my first inkling that I was a fearful person when I attended a church service and actually received a word from the Lord about it. It was during the worship part of the service when the music leader stopped singing and said, "I don't know who this is for and I don't usually do this but the Lord has impressed upon my heart that there is someone here that has a lot of fear; if you will come forward, God will set you free!" This went straight to my heart; I felt electrified on the inside. I knew that I knew that I knew God was speaking to me through this man. I just didn't know why God was telling me this? Why did God think I was full of fear, to the point that I needed to be set free? It wasn't as if I was afraid of my shadow all the time! I stood there gripping the pew in front of me as if it was a life raft and I was adrift on the sea. I knew God was trying to speak to me but I couldn't move. There was no way I was going to loosen my grip and go forward. What would people say if they knew I was the one full of fear?! As I held onto the pew for dear life, I wondered how anyone who was truly filled with fear could get the courage to walk up to the front of the church and let everyone know about it. The enemy kept me from moving forward to receive what God had for me that night but I did start thinking about fear and my reactions. Truth was starting to penetrate the invisible shroud of fear I wore but it would be several trips through this same storm before I could claim freedom. Thank God, He is the God of second, third, and fourth chances!

I Prayed For Boldness – Am I Sure I Really Want it??!

One of the most powerful testimonies I have ever heard in my life came from a woman by the name of Mary Kay Beard. Mary Kay shared about her life, specifically the time she had spent in prison. I wondered how in the world she could ever have the boldness and courage to do this; I would have died if anyone had known something like this about me. I sat there thinking about my past and how embarrassed I was about many of the things I had done. But the Holy Spirit was working through Mary Kay and He used her to provoke me into desiring and praying for freedom. Mary Kay had confidence, courage, and boldness, qualities that I did not have. Instead, I was fearful, intimidated, and prideful, cringing whenever I would run into people I knew from my old high school days. I came to learn that the situations from my past that I was most reluctant to share, most ashamed of, and most embarrassed about were the very things God would use to empower me to speak into others' lives. When the wind started to blow from the Spirit, He began to show me that covering up the past was not from Him and He wanted me free. And so I began to pray for boldness, holy boldness. What began as a prayer to be bold like Mary Kay turned into a journey with God, leading me through some seemingly treacherous valleys of death and then rivers of peace.

My first step in obtaining freedom from fear came from a very unlikely place. I had been taking a course in church called "master life" and Mary Kay was in our small group. At the end of the course, two people were asked to speak at a special event. These two people were chosen from all the small groups at church and were to speak on what their course had meant to them. "Yours truly" was one of the two. Yes, I was proud to be asked but I was scared to death. Oh Lord, why me? How in the world could I possibly do this? I began to pray and could see that this was God's way for me to have the boldness I had asked for. But I was still afraid and didn't want to do it. I was frozen with fear. What would these church people think of me? What if I said the wrong things? What if I couldn't remember what to say? I didn't even know what to say! I prayed and I prayed for boldness and the courage to do what I had been asked to do. The closer the time came for me to speak the more terrified I became.

I learned to listen to the Lord during this time more than I ever had before. I prayed as I would drive in my car and I would ask the Lord "what do You want me to say?" I don't think I had ever done this before. When thoughts started to come to my mind of little ideas, I knew these weren't my thoughts; they sounded so good. I jotted them down quickly and continued to pray. Soon that fateful night when I was to face the crowds came. With paper in hand, I walked to the front, praying with every breath "Lord, please give me the boldness I need to stand up here and please let these words be Your words -- not mine. Please speak through me, Lord." I physically shook the entire time I was speaking. I was afraid the folks in the audience would think I was having an epileptic fit or something. Afterwards I asked Arnold if he could see me shaking. He said he couldn't see me doing any gyrations up there but he could hear it a little in my voice. Arnold thought that I had done very well. My biggest supporter, however, was at the back of the room. When I was finished, I heard Mary Kay clapping loud and saying, "That's my sister! That's my sister!" To have the very person who had inspired me to pray for boldness present for my speech was an honor. To have her acting as my personal cheerleader was a reward from God.

The Giants Were Fear And Intimidation

I naively thought that I had conquered fear when I did my first public speaking after meeting Mary Kay. But God saw it differently and He was marching me forward. At first I didn't recognize the bad fruit of fear and intimidation in myself, until the Holy Spirit started to blow away some of the enemy's fog with a fresh wind of truth. One day the thought came to me, "If you can't say no to your children, then one day they will not be able to say no to theirs". The Word says to train up a child in the way they should go and when they are older, they will not depart from it (Proverbs 22:6). I asked myself, "what were my words, or lack of them, training my children to be? Was I fearful? Was I afraid to say no? Was I afraid to tell someone what was really on my heart for fear of hurting them? Was I intimidated or controlled by others? Was I looking for the approval of man? Was I doing any of the intimidating or controlling? Did I pass along any of this to my children? Where did all this come from, anyway?"

I knew that I had a hard time letting my yes be yes and my no be no. Many times I would do things I didn't really want to do and give when I didn't really want to give, in order to please OTHERS AND WIN THEIR APPROVAL. Up until now, I had thought I was not serving God and others if I told someone "NO". But God says to examine the fruit! This fruit might look pretty on the outside but it wasn't too pretty on the inside. An insecure person will have a hard time delivering the word "No". After all, someone may reject me if I don't please them or do things their way. But I wanted to change my ways and let the Holy Spirit, not man, lead me! I began to ask God to help me truthfully answer all these questions and to show me what to do about them. Right off the bat, God told me that if I do something I don't really want to do in order to please someone other than Him, then I am letting fear and intimidation rule over me; I have given that person too much control over with my life.

My Bank Account Was Set Up at an Early Age

I began to examine my past, those early years, to see where the seeds of this fruit had come from. I realized that fear was instilled in me at a very early age. My daddy was always the "life of the party" and loved to joke and tease with everyone. However, the fun he might have intended towards me produced only fear, not laughter. It was **AWFUL!** Daddy would hide outside, jump out from behind a bush when I was going by, and scare the daylights out of me. Many times daddy would hide behind my door or in my closet and jump out and scare me when I opened it. I also loved to watch scary movies in my younger years. When the lights were out, my imagination would run wild.

Looking back, I realized that mom and I walked on eggshells a lot of the time around my daddy because he had a rather explosive temper. I can still remember the many times mom would say "don't say a word to your daddy, you know how he is". We were both intimidated by him. Fear certainly had time to establish quite a root system in my heart, mind, and thoughts!

She Was A Woman Of Worth

But God was applying the "Round-Up" to this weed in my life. God's weed-kill would take care of what the enemy had planted and cultivated! God used a situation at work to show me how fear was allowing me to be controlled by other people. When I was young, I didn't have a very good work ethic. To me, work meant doing what I was told to do and that was it; I would do the least I could get away with and usually with drudgery. But the good work ethic from mom and dad began to kick in somewhere along the line and I began to see that working hard was something I could take pride in. I had been working at a store part-time; one of my co-workers seemed to have the same tactics that I did when I was younger. This super nice young woman had a lot of worth as a person. She liked the customers and they seemed to like her. But when it came to going the extra mile and helping me with keeping the store clean and looking good, she was nowhere to be found.

The Holy Spirit told me that I should confront her and not fear her. "Oh no", I thought, "there's no way I'm going to talk to her about what's bothering me." But the Holy Spirit continued, "You are the one having the problem with her. Why are you afraid to confront her?" Was I truly afraid to confront her? Why did I feel so hesitant in sharing what was bothering me. God showed me that I felt this way because I was fearful of her response. What if she got mad? What if I make her feel bad and hurt her? I prayed and prayed some more. Thoughts began to come to mind of what I needed to say to her concerning how I felt I was doing most of the work. "Lord, how in the world can I do this? God, would You give me the courage and boldness that I need to do this?" I knew my answer was not in going to the manager about this or stuffing it inside of my heart any longer. My answer came by going to the Father, asking Him for a confident heart, and allowing myself to be led by the Holy Spirit.

I had decided that the next time I worked with her would be D-day. I wasn't going to allow this to stay inside me any longer. I couldn't believe how fearful I was. As I worked, I prayed that the Holy Spirit would take away my fear; give me courage and the right words to say. "Oh Holy Spirit, please give me Your boldness." When I spoke to her and shared what had been bothering me, it was as if life was pouring into me. Storing, or rather stuffing, these thoughts inside of me was not producing life at all. When I finished she was very nice and told me she had no idea that I had felt that way. By her humble apology, I realized that she was a woman of worth; with true humility she received my gentle correction and did not seem to resent it or me. God was definitely with me in this storm; He gave me the courage to confront!

Later that morning the Lord spoke something else to me concerning fear. Thoughts began to come to mind of a bear in the woods and one of those big metal traps that had huge teeth in them. If the bear gets its leg caught in the trap, he slowly bleeds to death. "This", the Lord spoke to me, "is what happens when you let yourself be controlled by fear. It is the enemy's way of letting you bleed to death, Wanda." God was setting me free and pulling the plug on the enemy. With the Holy Spirit breathing on me and bringing His wind of truth, I was getting free from where the enemy had me trapped!

She Was Trapped By Fear, too!

One day while I was waiting in the doctor's office, I started talking to a young woman who was also waiting. One thing led to another and before long, we were talking about the trap she was in with her mother. It seems mama hadn't quite cut the apron strings and wouldn't even let her grown daughter go to the store without her. The young woman went on to tell me how she had even tried one day to go to Wal-Mart without telling her mother. Mama somehow got wind of it and when this wind blew, so did mama and over she came to Wal-Mart! This young woman said that her mother wanted to know what she was doing there without her?! While the young woman shared her heart with me, she seemed so hopeless, as if there was no chance for change. Talk about control! Intimidation! Fear to Confront! This young woman was married with children but was afraid to tell mama what was really on her heart! Imagine! This poor, trapped woman!

Deceived No More!

Was God trying to show me something? Was He trying to show me a reflection of my life through this woman? "Lord, show me any and every place where I am fearful" became my heart's cry. "Holy Spirit, please bring me truth and insight." He certainly obliged. As I prayed, God began to show me where I was fearful and deceived. I had a frightful dream one night. In the dream, I was working on a project when all of a sudden a car pulled up and parked nearby. A man got out and started to walk towards me. Another car pulled up and then another. Several men and even women got out of the cars and started walking towards me. Before I knew it, I was surrounded by these strangers. I could tell that they wanted to do something evil to me and I had the sickest feeling I was about to be attacked and raped. I was frozen with fear; I didn't run or leave; I just stood there and watched them get closer and closer.

When I woke up, I immediately asked the Lord for the interpretation of this horrible dream. As I sat there shaken and waiting for His answer, I realized how horrible it must be when something like this really happens to someone; the fear and terror in him or her must be horrendous. I didn't have to wait long. God whispered these thoughts to my mind: "When you can't say no to people, this is when you are abused, Wanda. This is when you can be raped by man." I had started out by believing a lie. A deception from the enemy that told me I was to do everything for everyone, even when my heart was telling me "NO". I had been thinking I was doing a "Godly" thing when I would say "yes" to lots of things and to lots of people. But God wanted me to know how very wrong I was and how subtle the enemy can be. In trying to keep people happy, I was really destroying myself, at times. I don't want anyone who has actually been abused or raped to think that if they had just said NO or walked away that this wouldn't have happened to them. This dream was just God's way of showing me what was happening to my heart when I wouldn't say "NO" out of fear of their response.

Get Up and Get Dressed!

I had an opportunity to see the enemy and his plan stopped one day, thanks to the Lord reminding me of His Word in Jeremiah 1: 17-19. The Lord told me that I was to get up and get dressed and not be afraid of anyone. "Why the warning, Lord?" "What am I going to be doing?" The thought had been coming off and on to take a copy of a Psalms 91 card and give it to a particular Jewish woman! God had put a special place in my heart for this Jewish woman, even after being told that she cursed the last person who witnessed to her. With fear and trembling in my heart, I knew what I had to do: give her the Psalm 91 card anyway! I was gently reminded by the Holy Spirit, as I struggled with fear, "you are accountable to God, Wanda, not to man". I knew it was God that I needed to please! Timidity, Fear, and Pride HAD TO GO! Soon I had my chance. As I stood before this Jewish woman, fear tried to come in and I found myself trying to reason, "this is not the right time! She's so hard! She won't receive this! You know what she said to the last woman who witnessed to her; it's not going to do any good!" And then I heard the word that the Holy Spirit was bringing to my mind. Deuteronomy 31:6 'Fear not, nor be afraid of them, for I AM WITH YOU!' **If God is for me, who cares who isn't!!!** I decided I'd better listen to the voice of the Holy Spirit and quit worrying so much about how this woman was going to respond! I pulled the Psalms 91 card out of my purse and handed it to her, finding myself sharing with her how the soldiers of the 91st brigade had prayed this scripture every day during World War 1. This brigade engaged in three of the wars' bloodiest battles. Other units suffered up to 90% casualties, but the 91st brigade did not suffer a single combat related death. She nodded without saying a word, took the card from me and then she left.

It was over! I did it! God had given me the courage to walk over the plans of the enemy to keep me silent. I was also reminded of another thought: "Fear strung its chord to sing its song, and then faith walked over them!" That is the faith in my God to be with me, no matter what!

I prayed that what I had said to her would bear fruit, knowing I might not ever know. I still see her from time to time but she never mentions the scripture card. I don't know if confronting her with God's Word was for her as much as it was for me to be set free from the fear of another person's opinion of me. But I knew one thing: courage does not mean the absence of fear; it means I'll go forward even if fear is there! I believed God's promise for me and He was faithful to fulfill it!

Letting Someone Always Have Their Way Was Not Being A Helpmate!

I had been praying that God would set me free from fear to have my own mind. I had never thought about that before until the Holy Spirit brought to my mind one morning that I was to break off all mind control from my life. What mind control? As the Holy Spirit brought light to another dark place, He showed me that both Arnold and I were to think for ourselves and voice our own thoughts and opinions, yet in such a way as to honor one another in love and mutual respect.

Freedom to think for myself and have my own opinion rather than just going along with Arnold was a new way of submission in my house. I had been totally off base in God's eyes concerning this thing. I was to have a mind of my own and one way God would show me would come through my new car. Arnold and I had been talking about getting me a new car and I was thrilled. Arnold told me exactly what we could afford and we set a price limit. He is terrific with finances. Thanks to him and the wisdom God gives him, we have managed to stay out of debt. But I could feel the air leak out of my newly inflated tires when Arnold started telling me the kind of car **he** wanted me to have and why **he** had picked out this particular one! God, what do I do? What do I say? I don't want a car like that. I didn't want to seem ungrateful; after all, I had been praying for months with all my heart that God would give me a "THANKFUL HEART"! And now I wasn't thankful at all but acting like an ungrateful child. I soon realized that was not true; I was just beginning to realize my own mind. God would show me exactly what I was supposed to do once I prayed and asked Him.

I remembered that God had given Gideon (Judges 6 & 7) a plan to defeat the enemy in his life and I wanted God's thoughts and plan to defeat this fear and intimidation, too. So I prayed and I asked the Lord to bring to mind His insight and wisdom where this car situation was concerned. "Lord, am I being selfish or is there something You're trying to show me here?" All sorts of thoughts of when Arnold had gone to purchase his van began to come to mind. The research on the internet, the checking of the paper, and the excitement as he looked for just the one he wanted was on the replay button of my mind. I had not picked out Arnold's van; he had. He experienced joy when looking for what he wanted and could afford. God was showing me in looking back that there was nothing wrong with me wanting the same excitement in looking and finding my favorite car, too. I kept sitting there and saying "God speak to me. Show me what You want me to do." With those words no sooner out of my mouth, a thought came to mind: "I already have! I just showed you what Arnold did and that it is alright for you to have the same fun in finding your own car." I was finding out that praying first concerning Arnold or any other situation would bear much fruit. I said to the Lord, "God show me Your timing and prepare Arnold's heart to receive what I am going to say." At first, Arnold was a little reluctant but God was doing a work in my husband's life, also. Instead of being stubborn and hardheaded, he was humble and attentive. The pride was vanishing in both of us. Thank You, God!

I told him I wanted a Volkswagon bug, and so the search for one began. Arnold began his search in the newspaper and looked for what I wanted just like he had done for the van. As it turned out, the very first car that Arnold had seen in the paper was what we finally bought. When we drove up onto the car lot, I knew "this one's for me". It was an adorable, soft green and had only 5000 miles on it. Even my mom loves this car and feels like a kid in it when I pick her up to run errands.

Speaking My "Peace"

God revealed another incident about having a mind of my own without feeling intimidated or guilty. I had always wanted to stop at a little spot that we would pass on our way to the beach. No special reason, my heart was just drawn there. It was just an ordinary spot that had a little road running down beside the bridge. As we drove by this spot on this particular beach trip, I told Arnold that I wanted to come back and see what was down that road before we left.

Arnold had gone to work that day and while we were eating dinner, I asked him if we could drive up there and get out and look around. At first, Arnold didn't seem to want to go but then said we would. I almost backed down and told him to forget it because he acted as though he really did not want to go. But I decided to be quiet for a change and say nothing; I was going to ignore his reaction to my request. God was trying to get through my thick head and deceived mind to show me that my desires were important, too. As we drove there, I realized it was much further down the road than I had remembered. Guilt started to consume me. Twice I almost said "forget it; it's too far"; "it's too much trouble", but I didn't. As it turned out, it was one of the most beautiful times we ever had at the beach. At this special spot that evening, Arnold and I watched a puppy run in and out of the water like some child with his family. We rolled up our pant legs and talked about how our "grand-dog", Fletcher, would love to do that. There were huge cranes all over the place and even a small pond filled with ducks over to one side. It was a private island paradise, just for us. I had almost missed this peaceful spot because I was afraid to speak what was on my heart, thinking I was not worth the time and effort to go there. The condemning heart would have to go; my thoughts of not being worthy were not from God!

My low self worth was beginning to ebb as my prayers concerning freedom from fear were increasing. I had prayed to see myself with value and honor, the way the Lord does. The more I looked to the Lord for my self worth, the more valuable I became in my own eyes. Devaluation cannot come when I look to God to get my sense of worth. Devaluation of self only comes when I accept man's opinion of my worth, rather than God's. Fear and intimidation were leaving as I prayed to have the mind of Christ, the perfect balance of submitting when I need to and boldly speaking my mind, as well.

Worry Was A Way Of Life! When I Trust Him, I'm Not Worried

I realized I had been worried and fearful about many things. Worry seemed to be a way of life for me. I felt fear when wondering, "what if my family does the wrong thing?" "What if they miss God?!" I had prayed about this one day and asked the Lord, "Why do I worry so much"? The thought that came to mind was **"Because you do not TRUST ME!"** God began to show me that when I really trust Him and when I have a fear of Him alone, that I would know He was quite capable of making changes in anyone when the time was right. Isaiah 8:12-13 was another word from God that I could trust Him: 'Do not be afraid that some plan conceived behind closed doors will be the end of you. Do not fear anything except the Lord Almighty. He, alone, is the Holy One. If you fear Him, you need fear NOTHING ELSE!' I had read scripture after scripture and found myself quoting, 'Do not be anxious, about anything' (Phil 4:6) and 'I command you; be strong and courageous. Do not be afraid or discouraged, for the Lord Your God is with you wherever you go!' (Josh 1:9) The fact that "In God We Trust" is on our dollar bills' backside didn't mean that I couldn't have it on my inside – inside of my heart! The people that had this printed on our money must surely have had a reason to put it there. But to be perfectly honest I was struggling with truly trusting God.

Let Love Find its Way, Lord: True Love is NOT Fearful!

At a church I had visited, I received a printed program with Bible scriptures on it about love. These scriptures were already familiar to me but somehow, this day, they really spoke to me. The one that really spoke to me that day was Romans 5:5. **'The Holy Spirit sheds abroad the love of God in your heart, Wanda'!** He Does? I had been asking and praying about love for years, like it was something that I was waiting on to just happen. I knew it was coming from God, but I did not know how He was going to send it or get it to me. I never thought of the Holy Spirit as having anything to do with love! I had stood in prayer lines and had prayed along with others for God's love to be released in my life, but I had never heard of the Holy Spirit helping me receive His love! I began to talk to the Holy Spirit about it, "Holy Spirit, come and shed abroad the love of God in my heart." I began to see little changes that I know weren't me and knew it must be the Holy Spirit working in me. I seemed to have more understanding! I was more patient and less fearful. I knew I had nothing to do with this change in me; only the Holy Spirit could come with his power and God's love to make these kinds of changes in me. God was driving out the fear with His perfect love, enabling me to trust Him even more! Revelations 21:5, **'Behold, God is making all things new! Even you, Wanda.'** The wind of the Holy Spirit was bringing revival to me and I was beginning to see. I realized that the Holy Spirit had been sent here to help me and I wanted all the help I could get from Him, everyday.

God began showing me all sorts of things about His love. Love, is not jealous! Love, does not control. Love is not filled with fear! 1 John 4:18 says 'There is no fear in love. But perfect love drives out fear. The one who fears is not made perfect in love.' I began to see, with all the fear that was in me, that love had not really found its perfect way in me. I realized that if I had that perfect love, I would not be so worried and fearful about things. As the Holy Spirit began to place God's love for me within my heart, my trust in Him grew. I realized that God loved me with a perfect love and that I could totally trust Him, 100%. **There would not be room for fear with a heart full of love and trust!**

We're Not To Fear Anyone Outside Of God!

One of my favorite stories in the Bible comes from Judges. (Judges 7:3) 'Remove all who are fearful! Send home any of your men who are timid and fearful!' Gideon was in charge of an army that was very out-numbered by the enemy's army. Gideon asked the Lord for a plan to overcome the enemy. The Lord told Gideon to remove those soldiers that had a fearful heart. Twenty-two thousand men left the army while ten thousand remained. Only those without fear could defeat the enemy. Fear is the first thing that has to go! These were words God spoke to Gideon and these were words the Lord gave to me. God was showing me once more that the fear of man had been a big trap and that houses built on fear, pride, or timidity were houses built on sand! Speaking truth would build our home on the solid rock – but it must be truth, spoken with love, God's perfect love!

When the wind blows and I stand up to fear, Jesus is having His way. The wind is symbolic of the Holy Spirit, as well as the destruction of the enemy. The wind that was blowing my way when I gave people too much control over my life was not from God! Even when I feel the wind is from the enemy, I pray and ask God to restore to me seven times what the enemy has stolen (Proverbs 6:31). I pray and I ask the Lord to show me how to take back and turn around the situation so that God is glorified and good comes from it. When the Holy Spirit begins to blow, it may be painful for a season but it's worth it. **When the Holy wind blows, new beginnings start; when the Holy wind blows, all sorts of buried treasures will be uncovered.**

I Will Give You A Gift!

God says that He gives me a GIFT -- peace of heart and peace of mind. John 14:27 says, 'Jesus said I am leaving you with a gift, peace of heart and mind, and the peace I give isn't fragile like the peace the world gives, so don't be troubled or afraid!' The fear of hurting someone or being hurt by someone kept me in prison! My fear of what man thinks or what woman thinks had such a hold on me; it put me in torment and caused me to lose my peace, but God was making me aware of it so I could be set free! In 1 Samuel 25:29 it says, 'Even when you are chased by those who seek your life, you are safe in the care of the Lord your God, secure in His treasure pouch! But the lives of your enemies will disappear like stones shot from a sling.' I pictured a mama kangaroo with her little one protected down inside her pouch and held close to her. This is how God protects me from the enemy. I am held safe and secure, close to Him; I can rest in total peace, without worry or fear. I prayed:

"Father, since the fear of man is a snare, I repent of that fear and renounce it, in the name of Jesus. I ask that Your perfect love, Father, cast out all my fears and fill me by Your sweet, Holy Spirit's power. I renounce pride from my life, that pride that would make me want man's approval and be fearful of what they would think. And I place upon myself a new coat today, a coat worn by Jesus, a coat of humility. (Colossians 3:12) I place upon myself a coat that covers me with compassion, kindness, humility, gentleness, and patience. I thank You, Father for Your peace that passes all of my understanding and the beautiful gifts of peace of heart and mind that Jesus said He would leave with me. I shod my feet with the gospel of peace and when the wind blows, I ask that You, the Lord, would be my strength and song and become my victory! (Exodus 15:2) Amen"

Scripture Used In This Chapter

Proverbs 22:6 Teach your children to choose the right path, and when they are older, they will remain upon it.

Jeremiah 1:17-19 "Get up and get dressed. Go out, and tell them whatever I tell you to say. Do not be afraid of them, or I will make you look foolish in front of them. For see, today I have made you immune to their attacks. You are strong like a fortified city that cannot be captured, like an iron pillar or a bronze wall. None of the kings, officials, priests, or people of Judah will be able to stand against you. They will try, but they will fail. For I am with you, and I will take care of you. I, the LORD, have spoken!"

Deuteronomy 31:6 Be strong and courageous! Do not be afraid of them! The Lord your God will go ahead of you. He will neither fail you nor forsake you.

Isaiah 8:12-13 Do not be afraid that some plan conceived behind closed doors will be the end of you. Do not fear anything except the LORD Almighty. He alone is the Holy One. If you fear him, you need fear nothing else.

Philippians 4:6 Don't worry about anything; instead, pray about everything. Tell God what you need, and thank him for all he has done.

Joshua 1:9 I command you--be strong and courageous! Do not be afraid or discouraged. For the LORD your God is with you wherever you go.

Romans 5:5 And this expectation will not disappoint us. For we know how dearly God loves us, because he has given us the Holy Spirit to fill our hearts with his love.

Revelations 21:5 And the one sitting on the throne said, "Look, I am making all things new!" And then he said to me, "Write this down, for what I tell you is trustworthy and true."

1 John 4:18 Such love has no fear because perfect love expels all fear. If we are afraid, it is for fear of judgment, and this shows that his love has not been perfected in us.

Judges 7:3 Therefore, tell the people, 'Whoever is timid or afraid may leave and go home.' Twenty-two thousand of them went home, leaving only ten thousand who were willing to fight.

Proverbs 6:31 But if he is caught, he will be fined seven times as much as he stole, even if it means selling everything in his house to pay it back.

John 14:27 I am leaving you with a gift--peace of mind and heart. And the peace I give isn't like the peace the world gives. So don't be troubled or afraid.

1 Samuel 25:29 Even when you are chased by those who seek your life, you are safe in the care of the LORD your God, secure in his treasure pouch! But the lives of your enemies will disappear like stones shot from a sling!

Colossians 3:12 Since God chose you to be the holy people whom he loves, you must clothe yourselves with tenderhearted mercy, kindness, humility, gentleness, and patience.

Exodus 15:2 The LORD is my strength and my song; he has become my victory. He is my God, and I will praise him; he is my father's God, and I will exalt him!

GREAT GUSTS OF PRIDE

Let Me Entertain You: The Zipper Story

(Romans 8:28) 'All things can and will work together for good to those who love the Lord…'. I cling to this verse when things happen in life that I don't understand or when I start thinking about things that have happened in my past, especially the times I'm not proud of or the times when I've really blown it. Sometimes a song or story will come to mind, along with the thought to share it; even though thoughts like this may not make much sense to me, I want the Holy Spirit to lead me. With that in mind, a song from an old movie reminded me of the work God was doing in my life. This movie was about a stripper who sang "Let Me Entertain You". That's right, a stripper! Remember, God can use all things, even our mistakes. Well, God was showing me that I needed to strip off a few layers of pride and self. Hebrews 2:14 tells us that only as a human being could Jesus have died and only by dying could He break the power of the devil who had the power of death. I needed to die to many things in order to break the power of the enemy off my life. And one way was by dying to my pride and what people would think of me.

I had a dream one night where I was wearing a jumpsuit that had a zipper all the way down the front. I dreamed that the zipper was totally unzipped and I was naked in front of a bunch of people. I was petrified, exposing myself in front of all these people! I kept thinking I needed to cover myself, after all, what would all these people think?!! When I awoke and thought back over the dream, I could only wonder why I didn't try to zip up the jumpsuit. I asked the Lord to show me the meaning to this dream. The thought came, "this is a good thing; in exposing yourself and being willing to share from your life's experiences, you're beginning to be real with people". Later, I started to share some of my weaknesses with people and was reminded that this was a good thing, not a bad thing. With God's help, I could be used to set others free. I had to put my confidence in the Lord's power, His Word, and His ability to handle things for me. I began to see that He would turn what Satan meant for bad into something good for me and possibly for someone else.

As I thought about the stripping away of pride, a recent trip to my dentist came to mind. I needed Novocain and then nitrous oxide just to clean my teeth because they were so sensitive. These would help to relax me, as well as ease the pain. I thought about how this was the way the Holy Spirit treated me; His "nitrous oxide and Novocain" helped numb the pain while He gently broke off the flaws and imperfections. He did this one layer at a time, just like the dental hygienist had done with the plaque on my teeth. In getting ready for the Lord's return this bride was in need of some repair; God was working and cleaning up the "pride plaque" on the walls of my heart. God hates pride, self-focus, and fear. Proverbs 6:16-17 says 'There are six things that the Lord hates, no seven things that He detests: Pride, lying, killing, a heart that plots evil, feet that race to do wrong, a false witness who pours out lies, and a person who sows discord among brothers.' He hated my pride just as much as the "big sins" of abortion, murder, adultery, etc.! When I truly humbled myself before Him, I realized that my sin, pride, is first in the list of things He hates. "Lord", I prayed, "let me see where I need to change and be set free." Little did I know the way God was going to reveal how much pride was in me!

The Wind Was Blowing At the Beach

Arnold and I had gone to the beach one week; he had work to do in the area and I was the trailing spouse. We decided on Sunday morning to take our quiet time on the beach. There are good winds, as well as bad ones, but the one blowing that day at the beach began to show me what I needed to see: THE TRUTH. The truth about the pride in me and where it was hidden. With beach hat, flip-flops, and shorts on, Arnold was ready to hit the sand and so was I. As we drove by this church, all of a sudden something happened to Arnold. He pulled into the parking lot of the church and told me that he's feeling led to attend this service. He says that he has a real desire to hear a good sermon that morning. While I'm sitting there frozen to the seat of the car, Arnold proceeded to open the door and get out. "This can't be real; this must surely be a joke" is all I could think. I thought one thing for sure, "THIS ISN'T THE LORD", or was it? This was the real deal and Arnold was serious. Well, in about one split second, "yours truly" got to see just how much pride was really in me. I was more concerned about what Arnold was wearing than what the service was going to be. I wouldn't budge. I just sat glued to the seat and told him I wasn't about to go in with him looking like that and if he wanted a sermon, I'd be glad to give him one when we got to the beach! If he wanted to go inside by himself that was fine, too. Needless to say, we didn't go to the service that morning, at least not the one being held in that church.

While we sat under the umbrella at the beach, I prayed and sought the Lord about what He wanted me to pray for our family. I began to feel the heat, not from the sun but from the Holy Spirit. The Holy Spirit began to convict me of how much pride I had. I ate a piece of humble pie that morning, as I prayed and humbled myself before God's face. I was seeking His forgiveness and asking Him to help me not to care anymore what someone thought. "Please help me to be happy that my man wanted to go to church" was my prayer that morning, as conviction ran all over me. I asked God to restore what 'the thief' had just stolen and show me a way I could get back a seven-fold return (Proverbs 6:31). The answer came with the thought to go back by the church that following Monday and purchase a tape of Sunday's sermon. I wasn't about to miss this divine message! On the way home, I listened to a good message on the tape but knew that the best message for me that day was from the Holy Spirit concerning how much pride was in me.

The Wind Was Blowing at the Church

God continued to get my attention. It seemed that there were many places where I had pride. I didn't even know there were so many places until the wind blew and God showed me what was hidden in the darkness within my own heart. We had gone to church one morning and at the end of the service, the pastor asked for anyone who wanted prayer to come forward. The service had been very moving.
Apparently my husband thought so, too, and went forward for prayer. While he was up there, I was sitting with the children and was thinking of Arnold. He was all alone at the altar and I decided I should go up there and STAND BY MY MAN, as they say. When I got near the front where Arnold was supposed to be, I looked down and closed my eyes, trying to be Holy, and slipped my arm around him. I began praying for my man, so I thought, and resting my head on his shoulder and giving him a little love squeeze. After several squeezes and prayers for him, I heard a little voice very gently nudging me with this thought: "This is not your husband".

My next thought was that this was not God's voice but the voice of the enemy and Satan is just trying to upset me at this very special time. I couldn't stand it any longer and decided to open my eyes and look at my husband. Absolute panic and terror began to rise up in me at what my eyes beheld. Sure enough, it was the voice of the Lord and He was really warning me to make sure I didn't give any more love squeezes to a complete stranger! As I looked at this man that I had been clinging to and loving on, I wondered how and when I made such a mistake. I noticed that he was tall like Arnold and had on a similar suit but where did he come from? I wanted to die and wished that a whale could have swallowed me, just like Jonah. I quickly excused myself, found Arnold, and slipped up into the arm of my man, all the time feeling sick, sick, SICK!

All the way back to our seats I kept dying inside, wondering WHAT WILL PEOPLE THINK? WHAT DID THAT MAN THINK?! This thought was followed by more godly ones: "I hope he never comes back to this church again; Lord, please never let me see this man again. Please let him forget what happened and not remember me!" When we sat back down in our seats, the first thing out of the kids' mouths was, "Mom, whoooo was that man?" I never knew what God did in Arnold's heart that day because I was so wrapped up in me and what I thought others might be saying about me. However, I do know that my heavenly Father was given a good laugh.

His Official Fault Finder

Arnold and I went to a friend's book signing at a very upscale establishment. Since Arnold was planning to go straight to the event from work, I packed him a nice outfit he could take along to change into at the store before leaving. I thought this would be much more appropriate than his existing work attire that would probably have cookie dough splattered on it by the end of the day. But Arnold didn't want to change his clothes; he wanted to wear what he had worn to work to the book signing. Well, that spirit of control, of witchcraft (manipulation) in me almost blew up inside because he wasn't wearing what I wanted him to wear. It seemed I still hadn't let my grown husband be all he wanted to be and God was not through with me yet, either. Even if it meant Arnold would wear a pair of pants with patches at the knees, I had to let what Arnold did or didn't do go! Why was it so hard for me to let him be who he wanted to be?!

So many times I had prayed for Arnold to get right, for God to straighten him out! As far as I was concerned, Arnold needed to be fixed. He wasn't nearly as spiritual as I thought he should be; he didn't pray as often or as long as I thought he should; and he wasn't putting God first in his life in the way I thought he should. My perception of a godly man was one that would spend at least an hour or two in prayer every day, always be witnessing to others about Jesus, hold a prominent place of leadership within the church, and be at every meeting he could possibly attend that pertained to God (prayer retreats, bible studies, conferences, etc.) Needless to say, he didn't meet my expectation of a spiritual leader and because he fell so short in this area, I frequently disregarded any "pearls of wisdom" from him. Since God had helped me resolve some issues concerning my spiritual walk, I felt that I was now in a place where I could help Arnold resolve some of his issues; I was now qualified to point out what needed fixing! I was trying to remove what I perceived to be the huge log from Arnold's eyes, not realizing I still had more planks in my eyes. Yes sir, Paul Bunyan was my new name! As much as I may have wanted it, I was not called to be my husband's official faultfinder. The Lord had called me to **respect** my man and what I wanted to do was correct him! The Holy Spirit would work with him; right now, the Holy Spirit was dealing with me!

God showed me that I had a log of pride that needed to be lopped off. Matthew 7:4-5 says "How can you say to your brother, 'Let me take the speck out of your eye,' when all the time there is a plank in your own eye? You hypocrite, first take the plank out of your own eye, and then you will see clearly to remove the speck from your brother's eye". God continued to change my perception of my husband as a spiritual leader and to help me focus on Arnold's good qualities. I was to release him from my expectations and desires and let him be all that God wanted him to be. As I began to pray about this, God began to show me what He saw in Arnold's heart; it was pure and humble. God began to show me that my man's heart was far more godly and pleasing than my definition of a godly man. With occasional thoughts of how stupid something was that he did or why he couldn't have done something my way, my Jezebel tendency was definitely showing. Oh, what a spirit of pride, control, and haughtiness that woman had and some of her was in me!

Don't You See My Shoes

One morning Arnold and I were getting ready to go to the mall and walk. I asked Arnold how much time we had before we left and he indicated we would leave in about 20 minutes. I decided to go out back and rake up a few more bags of leaves in the few spare minutes I had. I put on my grungy work shoes, a pair of black canvas slippers, and out the door I went. Arnold saw me go out the door and asked "you're all ready to go?" My first arrogant and haughty thought was to respond back with "Don't you see the shoes I'm wearing? These are my yard shoes, not my walking shoes!" But this time with the help of the Holy Spirit, I managed to choke the quick retort and responded with "No, I thought I would rake some leaves until you were ready to leave". As I raked up the leaves, the Holy Spirit brought to mind how He had put a halt to the plan of the enemy. The Holy Spirit also pointed out that I used to wish so badly that Arnold would realize how much he sounded like a smart aleck and here I was almost spouting some smart aleck response to Arnold. I wanted my garden to grow but I was the one planting the same unfruitful seed. "Nothing but weeds, Wanda; nothing but weeds is all you'll get with this kind of seed growing!"

First Things First

On another occasion, I remember being frustrated because I had a family member whose house was always a mess. I'd go over there to help her get the house cleaned up and before I could make it out the door, she had messed it up again. I sought the Lord and prayed for this person and felt God speak to my heart "Wanda, it's her heart that needs your prayers, that's the work that needs doing now." This wasn't the first time God had corrected me on this same issue, either. I was driving by a house in our neighborhood one day and was bothered by the mess I saw. Once again, the Lord spoke to me to pray for their hearts first. "You're more concerned with the outside of their house, Wanda, than you are with their hearts." God would remind me of other times when pride was in control. I had prayed for a divine appointment with a particular person but because my hair wasn't fixed, I wouldn't stop even though they were out in the yard at the moment I drove by! Or the time I threw out Arnold's favorite, raggedy shorts because I hated to think what people would say if he wore them in public (they were truly "holey" shorts but Arnold loved them). Why, oh why, was it taking me so long to get this lesson!

Garden of Weeds

All this time my focus had been on how much better things would be if others would change but God began to show me that I had all sorts of weeds that needed to be pulled from my own back yard. The Lord said, "Take care of your own weeds, Wanda". Why, oh why, did I always want to get at someone else's weeds?! Psalms 44:3 says 'they did not conquer the land with their swords; it was not their strength but the Lord's right hand'. It was by God's <u>mighty power</u> and because He <u>smiled upon them and gave them favor</u> that things would be different.

When I repent of some sin, whether it's pride, fear, unforgiveness or any other sin and I seek the Lord and turn from those evil ways, (by the power of the Holy Spirit) God will restore my back yard! I'm going to have roses growing back there rather than weeds!

Touched By An Angel

God has used movies, or a TV program like "Touched By An Angel" to speak to my heart and give me freedom that would have taken years to overcome through counseling. I remember a particular episode on TV of Touched by an Angel. The angel's name was Monica and she had a specific appointment time with God concerning a potential promotion. Monica was sidetracked trying to help a troubled girl and missed her appointment time with God. At the last moment the troubled girl exposed herself as really being an evil angel and Monica realized that she had been deceived. Monica ran out of the room and went to where the meeting was to have taken place. Tess, another angel, was there to comfort and encourage her but Monica was distraught because she couldn't get in to keep her appointment with God. Tess gave Monica some very good insight and wisdom and she told Monica that she didn't need to get into that room in order to talk to God; she could go to God herself and talk to him, anytime or anywhere. As Monica knelt on the ground to pray, the evil angel came up gloating over the fact that Monica didn't get to go meet with God but what she didn't realize was that Monica was about to enter the best room of all, the Holy room with God, right from where she was.

When Monica began to pray, my first thought was that Monica was going to seek the Lord to defend herself and tell God how she had been tricked and deceived by this wicked angel (this is what "yours truly" would have done). Monica brought to life a scripture I've read many times. 'Father, forgive them for they know not what they do' (Luke 23:34). When Monica prayed, she didn't pray for herself, she stood in the gap for the bad guy, the wicked angel who had deceived her! She prayed and cried out with such a **humble spirit** for this woman that it brought tears to my eyes. This angel touched my heart, because she prayed with **humility!** Her humble spirit broke something in me, and made me more and more aware of a haughty spirit of pride and how so much of the time my focus is on myself and where I have been wounded, where I have been offended, and where I have been hurt.

The evil angel started screaming when she heard what Monica was praying. You see, the enemy hates humility, but he loves pride. Good affects the evil one in a mighty way. It destroys his dark room where he develops all sorts of negatives like pride, fear, worry, and doubt; he even develops them free of charge! There was one more thing that Tess pointed out that touched me. She told one of the angels who was so religious and self righteous that God doesn't hate those who are evil, He pities them! I was convicted that I needed to pray for mercy and compassion, more than ever.

There was no contempt in Monica's voice, either. There was no pride and self-righteousness in Monica's tone as she prayed for her enemy; there was only mercy and pity for her. Monica truly had the heart of her heavenly Father. A destructive wind was trying to blow Monica away, but she humbled herself and she prayed! Could I learn from that, or what?! Monica knew that it didn't matter what others did to her in the light of what God had done for her. 'If I will humble myself, pray, seek God's face (not his hand all the time), and turn from my evil ways then God will heal my land'! (2 Chronicles 7:14) God did not say when others who are not saved get it right and get their act together. He said the church. God did not say when Wanda becomes a really good person and does good things all the time; He said that I am to humble myself.

This one TV episode was speaking volumes to my heart. God used this story to illustrate to me some needed truths.
Monica's attitude of prayer came from Proverbs 21:22: **The wise man conquers the strong man and levels his defenses!** Monica leveled the plans of the enemy by her attitude in prayer and in her heart. Monica exercised wisdom instead of retaliation; she wanted to see the misguided angel set free. This illustrated humility to me and how I am to pray for my enemies. A forgiving and humble spirit halts the plans of the enemy and de-thrones my pride. Jesus is my living example of humility. He cried out to God on behalf of those who mistreated him. So why couldn't I? Because pride was a biggie and had to be knocked out of my life.

There is a Balance

For years, my focus was consumed with the "outside of the cup" and what others would think of me. I wouldn't even walk from the house to the outside utility room to get the laundry if I wasn't dressed or my hair was a mess! Queen Esther was exquisitely groomed and coiffed before she went in to see the king and receive his favor. I wanted to look perfect at all times, just like Queen Esther. There are definitely valid reasons to look nice, but the problem I had went a little overboard. If God spoke and asked me to go, I would not leave the house until I was completely dressed and coiffed. God is setting me free and I love it. I still have a way to go until this flesh is totally dealt with and that will not be until I get to heaven, which is a "come as you are" party! Now, it is much more fun to laugh with my husband than to get all out-of-kilter concerning his mismatched clothes or when there is bird poop on my car and everyone else's car is clean. I can now experience joy when having people over, even if the yard is still not landscaped as I would like it to be. Arnold and I are enjoying the little things now and I am enjoying my new freedom but it's been a long process.

The Cure For The Pride Disease

Sharon Daughtery said that the Lord had shown her that pride was at the root of deception; deception meaning believing a lie. As I contemplated this statement, God directed me to Proverbs 2:3-4 'Cry out for insight and understanding. Search for them as you would for lost money or hidden treasures.' I wanted to be aware of the schemes of Satan and so I began to pray that the root of pride in me be renounced and cut off and the deception bound. When darkness comes to light the enemy has to flee. The more I prayed, the more I began to really "see"! Pride is very, very deceptive. Pride deceived me into thinking I was better than I actually was. Pride also deceived me into thinking that others needed to repent far more than I did. When I began to pray about pride in my own life, the Lord said "RENOUNCE IT! REPENT OF IT!" I discovered that if I disagree with someone to the point that I won't even listen to him or her then there's pride in my heart. But when I do listen to others, even when we disagree, I am walking in humility. I read a book by Andrew Murray called, "Humility". Murray said to "pray that God would make known to us and take from our hearts every kind and form and degree of pride, whether it be from evil spirits or our own corrupt nature. God would awaken in us the deepest depth and truth of that humility which can make us capable of His light and Holy Spirit." I recognized this prayer was for me and I pray it continually!

Isaiah 28:17 is a scripture that God used in describing our home to me and how things really were. 'I will take the measuring line of justice and the plumb line of righteousness to check the foundation wall you have built, Wanda. Your refuge looks strong but since it is made of lies, hailstorms will knock it down. Since it is made of deception, the enemy will come like a flood to sweep it away.' With God's help and the prayer from Andrew Murray, the truth was coming from the Holy Spirit; I was beginning to see why this scripture was for me. Pride was at the root of my deception and as I began to repent of the pride and ask God for His coat of humility, the Holy Spirit brought me truth and I began to see things differently. I wanted my prideful heart replaced by a humble heart. A humbled heart seeks praise from God, NOT FROM PEOPLE! My light bulb was increasing from a 40 watt to a 140 watt.

God spoke the best truth, the true cure to my prideful heart "I know you love me, Wanda, what I want you to know is how much I love you. That means no matter what you look like or how you sound when you sing, or how much you blow it or what other people think about you, I LOVE YOU!" I needed to know God loved me. As I prayed for God to continue to show me how much He loved me, I realized His love began to heal my wounds, the insecurities that had allowed deception and pride to take root. I wasn't nearly as quick to point out the faults of someone else; I began to look at my own heart first. He would make the changes in each of us, in His timing. Letting my man know how awesome he is to me and what I love about him is moving far more mountains than I could by trying to be his "official fault finder". I've had to pray "God, show me how You see Arnold. Show me what I could do or say that would bless and encourage him!" At times, it was really tough speaking those "good" words rather than pointing out the things that weren't right, but God wanted me to see and love Arnold like He does. As I began to see how much God really loved me, it became much easier for me to love and to see the goodness in others through a humble heart!

Scripture Used In This Chapter

Hebrews 2:14 Because God's children are human beings--made of flesh and blood--Jesus also became flesh and blood by being born in human form. For only as a human being could he die, and only by dying could he break the power of the Devil, who had the power of death.

Proverbs 6:16-17 There are six things the LORD hates--no, seven things he detests: haughty eyes, a lying tongue, hands that kill the innocent, a heart that plots evil, feet that race to do wrong, a false witness who pours out lies, a person who sows discord among brothers.

Proverbs 6:31 But if he is caught, he will be fined seven times as much as he stole, even if it means selling everything in his house to pay it back.

Matthew 7:4-5 How can you think of saying, `Let me help you get rid of that speck in your eye,' when you can't see past the log in your own? Hypocrite! First get rid of the log from your own eye; then perhaps you will see well enough to deal with the speck in your friend's eye.

Psalm 44:3 They did not conquer the land with their swords; it was not their own strength that gave them victory. It was by Your mighty power that they succeeded; it was because You favored them and smiled on them.

Luke 23:34 Jesus said, "Father, forgive these people, because they don't know what they are doing." And the soldiers gambled for his clothes by throwing dice.

2 Chronicles 7:14 Then if my people who are called by my name will humble themselves and pray and seek my face and turn from their wicked ways, I will hear from heaven and will forgive their sins and heal their land.

Proverbs 21:22 The wise conquer the city of the strong and level the fortress in which they trust.

Isaiah 28:17 I will take the measuring line of justice and the plumb line of righteousness to check the foundation wall you have built. Your refuge looks strong, but since it is made of lies, a hailstorm will knock it down. Since it is made of deception, the enemy will come like a flood to sweep it away.

A JEALOUS WIND BLOWS

Jealousy Goes Real Well, Right Between The Butter And The Jam

God was taking me to another part of my "house" that needed a good cleaning; this dirty room was called jealousy. I was having a conversation with Arnold at breakfast one morning, and by the way, breakfast is such a good time to share your petty problems! It goes so well right between the butter and the jam, creating such a nice case of indigestion. I decided that this was the morning to open up and share something with Arnold that had been bothering me. After I had finished, he decided it was his turn. Arnold said he had kept quiet for all of these years, but now was the time for him to share what had been bothering him, too. Arnold told me that I was jealous and had been jealous for as long as he could remember. He said that it really bothered him even from the beginning of our relationship but had decided he would keep it to himself. It was like the floodgates had opened up. All this stuff came spewing forth. I was almost speechless...but not quite. My last words to Arnold as he walked out of the house were, "I'm going to pray about this. I don't want this in my heart, IF IT'S TRUE!"

Me? Jealous??!!

My prince, it seemed, was not like I wanted him to be. I wanted Arnold all to myself, his eyes only on "yours truly". I wanted to supply him with all he would ever want to look at and I tried my best to make him see just me. But all I was doing was getting myself upset and turning him against me. It seemed to me that after we got married, I was no longer the princess. I felt more like the poor sister back at the cabin washing the dishes and waiting on people. Why didn't he treat me like a princess anymore? I prayed about this and asked the Lord if I had any jealousy in me. The Lord brought to mind one simple thought; "yes, you have jealousy in your heart"! Oh, no! How do I pray about this? How do I get rid of it? It's one thing to know I have a problem and it's another thing to find out how to get rid of it. This thought came to mind <u>"cut off the source that's supplying the root with</u>

<u>its energy</u>". To receive this insight from the Holy Spirit was one of those light bulb moments for me.

I never used to think about having jealousy. I thought everyone was jealous, being jealous was ok, a normal emotion. If I felt jealous then it must mean I loved that person deeply. But what did the Lord have to say about it? What was the Word saying to me? I Corinthians 13:4 said, 'Love is patient! Love is Kind! And what it is not, JEALOUS!' Just like that. I knew what the Lord said and I didn't want this unwelcome houseguest anymore.

The Thorns of Wanda

As I sat there thinking about my jealous behavior throughout different times in my life, God began to show me who had been a thorn in my life. Remember the Rose of Sharon; well these women were The Thorns of Wanda! A woman that worked with Arnold would occasionally tell me that she and Arnold did something together at work or that she had talked to him three times that day while he was out of town. I, of course, would have only talked to him once that day. It would go all over me! I hated what I was feeling, but I couldn't seem to control the sick feeling that would wash over me. And then there was the time that this "thorn" told me about not being able to go and do stuff because she didn't have a babysitter. I didn't think anything about it until she started laughing and told me that she thought I might baby-sit since I didn't work and had plenty of free time. I had to pray and pray a lot about that one.

Another thorn came to mind as I thought about the torment throughout the years that the enemy had put me through. This thorn was a real doozie. She knew how to be coy and cute, and she was always playing up to my man; he just couldn't see it. While Arnold and I were in New York, he had to work with this particular cutie pie. One night he came back to the motel he informed me that we would be having dinner with all of the women he was working with that day. He said he hated to see them going to dinner by themselves in New York.

I found myself fuming especially where "the Thorn" was concerned, and it was all I could do to keep from blowing up! Why couldn't Arnold just take me?!! That evening at dinner, I know my annoyance was showing. I don't remember what I said, but it was obvious that I wasn't too thrilled that this thorn was robbing me of time alone with my Romeo. She knew it too and played it for all it was worth, "oohing" and "aahing" at every word he said and what they had done that day and how funny this and that was. I was getting madder and madder as each minute went by. Arnold was just lapping it up, positively glowing in the light of all the attention. If I had wanted Arnold to know how wonderful he was, I could have told him. I sure didn't need her to do that for me.

After dinner, we went back to the hotel and I began packing. I got my bag packed and a few choice words under my belt of what I thought about our night. I was hurt and I was furious! Around 2:30 that morning, I was in a cab heading for the airport. I had decided that I was not going to stay there with Arnold a minute longer and was going to just leave him in New York! But about halfway to the airport, I realized I wasn't alone in that cab, the Lord was there with me. Before I knew it that still small voice was urging me to tell the driver to take me back to the motel. Arnold and I did make up in the very wee hours of that morning but I was not a very happy person on this trip. In fact, this attitude continued for the next few years, too, as long as jealousy was still in my heart.

I was even jealous of my ex-husband and his family. In the early years of my marriage to Arnold, the children (Franklin and Rebecca) would go to their dad's house for the weekend. They would frequently come home with stories of the new house, or the new car, or the fact that their stepsiblings got three times more presents for Christmas than they did. I would get so angry and feel like I was dying inside. It would just about kill me; all I could think about was when I was married to their dad, we had only a small rental house. We even had to move in with my parents after Rebecca was born to save money! Why was his new family getting all these blessings??!!

The Lord was bringing to light all sorts of hidden places. I remember finding myself feeling jealous and resentful when a particular singer would come on television. To me she was unattractive but her voice was awesome and my husband didn't seem to think she was so bad to look at. In fact, he would light up like a Christmas tree when she would appear on some TV special. He would just seem to be awe struck and would go on and on about her voice and the way she could sing. All I could do was sit there and think, "He never wants to hear the songs the Lord has given me. Why, he didn't even ask about listening to the last song I recorded! Shouldn't my man stand by me and 'ooh' and 'aah' when I'm singing? Shouldn't he be my greatest fan?! Why, oh why, wasn't he sitting up and noticing me like that?"

Hand in hand with jealousy comes competition. I would actually compete with Arnold to see who could finish a task quicker or better! Love is not jealous or competitive but I certainly was. I would watch others say great things about him and sit back wondering to myself, "what about me and the wonderful things I do?!!" I would always want Arnold to notice what I had done; I did my best to point them out rather than to comment or care about what he had done. The competitive spirit was definitely not from God and it was not making my man or my house stronger.

Milk, Good for the Bones!

Jealousy, it says in the Word, "rots the bones" (Proverbs 14:30). So what was I supposed to do about it? Take extra calcium?? I began one of my favorite ways to find out about something -- look in the book and pray! Get those scriptures concerning that particular problem I'm dealing with (pride, fear, or whatever) and ask the Holy Spirit to let the ones that specifically are for me, stand out! The enemy was continuing to steal from me until I realized that jealousy was rotting **my** bones. I was tired of having the enemy huffing, puffing, and blowing my house down. I wanted a house built out of brick, not hay and sticks! The rock of ages, Jesus Christ, was my solid rock and my new beginning. With prayer, patience and lots of the love from the Holy Spirit, there were going to be some changes made.

Jealousy, I soon realized, had many friends. Fear was at the root of my jealousy. I had fear that I would lose my man; fear that he wouldn't love me anymore, and fear that someone would steal him from me. A footnote in my Bible concerning Genesis 27:41 says that jealousy causes blind anger. I could see this was true about my jealousy. Whenever I felt Arnold's focus shift from me to some other woman, anger would start to rise up in me. I wanted all of his attention and would get angry if I didn't get it. Genesis 13:7&8 shows that jealousy can tear believers apart. That was sure true! These jealous feelings had torn me apart, and made me so suspicious and uncomfortable when I was around particular women. If Arnold would look over at them or be extra nice to them, (nicer than I thought he was to me) then bingo, the giant had struck a home run again! The caption for Genesis 26:12-

16 indicates that jealousy is a strong dividing force. Yep, that was right on because Arnold told me that it had pushed him away from me.

I also read that jealousy leads to criticism; this sure fit Miriam's profile. Moses' choice of a wife gave Miriam, his sister, an opportunity to criticize (Numbers 12). Miriam's insecurity caused her to become critical towards Moses. Now I was beginning to see from the Word what this jealousy was doing to me. I could also see that the critical spirit in me was springing forth from all my insecurities.

Living Like A Philistine

The Word (Genesis 26:12-16) says that Jehovah blessed Isaac with tremendous grain, flocks of sheep, goats, cattle and many servants; so much so that the Philistines became jealous of Isaac. Ouch! I had become jealous because of someone's money, position, knowledge, talents, and even gifts from God. I usually compared myself to others around me, found fault with myself, and grumbled a whole lot because I didn't have the talents, degree, or job that someone else had. I was a housewife. I didn't have a degree in anything and never excelled in school. When I was a kid, I thought that the best thing that could ever happen to me was to grow up, get married, have a couple of kids, and live happily ever after. When I got married, I was very insecure and was always comparing myself to others. I would get especially insecure when Arnold talked about someone he respected that worked outside the home. I didn't want to work outside the home; I loved my home and my heart was here. I would work so hard trying to get Arnold to notice what I had done around the house but his lack of attention on my work here and his obvious displeasure at no paycheck coming in from me made what I did seem to be of little value and importance. With a jealous heart, I would look at other women and what they were doing and wish I had an important career. I would feel sick and so inadequate when I looked at these women with the so-called important roles in life. The ones who were making the money seemed to be better women since they were doing something to make a difference, something that would really count. I was like the Philistines, jealous of other's blessings!

Now that I knew the truth about what God said about jealousy, I didn't want it as my sidekick anymore. I wanted to be free of this torment. I was at the store working one day when one of my thorns showed up again. I don't remember what she said this time but I do know that I recognized the torment that the enemy was about to put me through with her and I went the other way and prayed, "Lord would You cut off the source that's supplying the root with its energy". I didn't know what the root was but I knew what the source was and I wanted this enemy bound from having any more control over me. "Holy Spirit", I said, "would You come with Your power and help me", and He did!

I didn't want to feel anger or threatened by anyone. I began to speak the Word from 1 Corinthians 13:4, remembering that this was the way that Jesus defeated the enemy when He was in the wilderness by speaking the Word. 'Love is patient and kind and it is not jealous.' The Word was working and I knew God was doing something even if I didn't feel all of the symptoms leaving at once. I began to feel more comfortable when one of my old thorns was around. I prayed and asked the Lord to bring to light every place in me that needed to be exposed. I prayed more than once "God help me hate what You hate and love what You love". With continued prayer, the fear started to lessen, the pride began to crumble, and jealousy started to leave. I didn't just wake up one morning and start hating the fear, the pride or the jealousy in me. I had to wait before the Lord and pray with all of my heart that He would expose and bring to light the things that were not right in me. And He did; one lesson at a time.

God-given Talent

When I started getting free from jealousy, I was so thankful. It was so nice to sit and listen to someone sing and appreciate their talent and gift from the Lord without becoming sad, mad, depressed, and jealous over it. Comparing and jealousy was definitely robbing me of God's best. God began to show me that He had made me the way I was and though I didn't have a paycheck, I was equally important in my role as a wife and mother. Then one day He began to open my eyes to the talent He had given me, to make our home a delightful place to live. It was fruitful, beautiful, and full of witty ideas and bargains He had helped me find. He had given me a talent for making our tent into a beautiful castle. He reminded me that His love wasn't jealous and He would show me how to make the most with what we had to work with and that it would be beautiful. "Just focus on what I've given you, Wanda. Pray for your talents to increase and don't compare your talents to anyone else's talents".

Vice Versa

One night I had a dream where a woman stabbed me three different times. When I got up that morning, my first thought was one of danger and to pray for my protection. For the first time in my life, I could relate to how someone might feel who has been stalked. I immediately told Arnold about my dream. I didn't know the woman in my dream but Arnold told me whom he thought the woman represented. It was someone I actually knew although I didn't recognize her in my dream. We prayed, asking the Lord to turn topsy-turvy the plans of the enemy for my life. I continued to pray about this throughout the morning and this thought came to mind, "she's jealous of your work." Here I was with a jealous and competitive spirit and someone was jealous of me! I found myself saying, "Come Holy Spirit with Your power and cut off the source that supplies the root with its energy". I began praying for this woman, asking the Holy Spirit to come with His power to set her free, just like I had prayed for myself.

Love Was Not Jealous, So Why Was I?

If love is not jealous and I was, then I was still missing some bricks. I began to pray that God would reveal His love for me and to me! This is probably a girl thing, but I remember taking a flower and pulling off the petals and saying, "he loves me, he loves me not". And then when I got to the end, whichever one I was left with was the one that determined whether he did or did not love me. Well, I was always so thrilled when it would land on "He loves me" and not so happy when it didn't, as if that really meant it was true or not.

God loves me, regardless. He loves me, in spite of! God's word says 'I love Him, because He first loved me' (1 John 4:19), but it never really dawned on me what this actually meant. I never did really understand His loving me, and then I realized one day that I really needed to know about God's love for me. I needed to believe that He loved me no matter what I looked like or what my lot in life was. I needed to be healed from all the false kinds of love that the world had offered! I needed my emotions repaired, as well as my distorted view of the definition of true love. One step at a time, God began to reveal His love to me through His Word. Psalm 127:3 says 'Children are a gift from the Lord; they are his reward from Him.' I would quote this off and on to others to show them they were from the Lord. They were His reward, not some wart on a frog. Well, one day God let me see what I had prayed for them was for me, too. I can remember the Holy Spirit speaking to me and prompting me to speak the word out loud. I began to speak, "I am God's gift. I am His reward!" By the third or fourth time of speaking this aloud, I could feel my turkey feathers leaving and new eagle feathers forming. I was loved! I was God's gift and I was made in His image and likeness. I began to feel power and life coming into me as I spoke His Word and **believed** it was for me, too.

The thought came to mind that I needed to pray for love to find a way in me or it just wouldn't happen. "God, reveal to me how much You really love me" was my prayer for others but now it was for me. We receive not, because we ask not, is what the Lord says (James 4:2-3). The thought came to make a card with a rose on it and print and laminate the words: **He loves me.** I prayed to receive a revelation of His love by the Revelator Himself - the sweet, precious Holy Spirit who reveals all sorts of things.

A revelation of God's love for me was my first insight into the BIGGER PICTURE! The Holy Spirit's wind was blowing the dirt and lies of the enemy away from our house. Defeating the enemy, as someone once said, was definitely not a power struggle of whose power was greater, but a truth encounter. The Holy Spirit wanted me to know I was loved. **And God's truth was when I had His love in me and knew how special I was to Him then I would not be jealous.**

A Grateful Heart

Colossians 3:23-24 says that 'whatever we do, do it as unto the Lord and not unto men. Knowing that you will receive your reward for your service to the Lord Jesus.' The Lord woke me up one morning and showed me that my focus was wrong. The Holy Spirit began to whisper to me "be content with what you have". I started praying that I would become more thankful and that God would give me a new, thankful heart. More and more I was seeing that changes all start with the heart! He was restoring and answering my prayers. I was learning to be more content with who I was and by doing so, I was not jealous of someone else, his or her position, or whether or not I had been noticed. I was even more content with Arnold.

As the Lord spoke to my heart one morning, He gave me these morsels to munch on. "Compare yourself with no one! I made you the way that you are. The talents I gave you are your talents, just the ones I created specifically for you. And that goes for your personality, too. I didn't make you to have a talent like someone else". There's nothing like having a kid who won't be grateful and I wasn't very grateful to my heavenly Father for the way He had made me. After I began to pray, I began to like my personality, my talents, and my house. I was becoming content with what I already had and who I was -- just happy He had made me. Whenever I started to focus on what was not right with me, I would stop, stand and tell Satan "NO!" And then I would thank the Lord for every blessing I could think of, which were many, and for making me just the way I am!!

The more God's love was filling me by the power and truth from the Holy Spirit, the more I was being set free. And Arnold wasn't worrying about whether I was going to get upset by him speaking to some other woman or looking at them in a way I didn't think he should. If Arnold is doing something he's not suppose to be doing, God sees him and if he's wrong, God will show him. I'm only responsible for me. I know one thing: a man thinks a whole lot more of a woman who knows who she is in Christ than he does of a woman who is jealous and obsessed by her insecurities! I was glad to be me and so happy to be free! Isaiah 54:11 was coming true for me because I was beginning to see and be thankful for who I was and not what I wished I could be. 'O storm battered city, trouble and desolate, I will rebuild you on a foundation of sapphires and make the walls of your house from precious jewels. I will make your towers of sparkling rubies and your gates and walls of shining gems.'

To abide satisfied meant I had to be grateful for what I already had; complaint department no longer open! Wanting more had been a way of life with me. Greed had set in at an early age. With never enough clothes or toys, I always wanted and had to have more. God showed me that being content was powerful. It would bring me peace, no matter what I did or didn't have. And it would lead me beside the still cool waters. I started praying and asking the Lord to help me be content whether I had everything I wanted or not. I repented of the greed and prayed that God would replace it with mercy. To abide satisfied created a peace within me that nothing in this world could ever satisfy.

"Lord, I bind greed from my life and I repent of it. I ask that You would help me to be content with what I have and to show me whenever greed does try to take over. My desire, Lord, is to be like Paul; content no matter what situation I'm going

through. Lord, give me a heart of GRATITUDE. I want to be grateful and thankful for all the things You have given me. Lord, I break the pride within me that makes me think I deserve better or more. In Jesus name, AMEN"

Scripture Used In This Chapter

Proverbs 14:30 A heart at peace gives life to the body, but envy rots the bones. (NIV Translation)

Genesis 27:41 Esau hated Jacob because he had stolen his blessing, and he said to himself, "My father will soon be dead and gone. Then I will kill Jacob."

Genesis 26:12-16 That year Isaac's crops were tremendous! He harvested a hundred times more grain than he planted, for the LORD blessed him. He became a rich man, and his wealth only continued to grow. He acquired large flocks of sheep and goats, great herds of cattle, and many servants. Soon the Philistines became jealous of him, and they filled up all of Isaac's wells with earth. These were the wells that had been dug by the servants of his father, Abraham. And Abimelech asked Isaac to leave the country. "Go somewhere else," he said, "for you have become too rich and powerful for us."

1 Corinthians 13:4 Love is patient and kind. Love is not jealous or boastful or proud

1 John 4:19 We love each other as a result of his loving us first.

Psalm 127:3 Children are a gift from the LORD; they are a reward from him.

Colossians 3:23-24 Work hard and cheerfully at whatever you do, as though you were working for the Lord rather than for people. Remember that the Lord will give you an inheritance as your reward, and the Master you are serving is Christ.

Isaiah 54:11 O storm-battered city, troubled and desolate! I will rebuild you on a foundation of sapphires and make the walls of your houses from precious jewels.

A BITTER GALE OF UNFORGIVENESS

Rescued From Darkness, He Turned On My Light!

I listened to some wonderful teaching tapes by Joyce Meyer on leadership. Joyce taught on several "negative" conditions of the heart and I realized that I had many of them. I definitely had the offended heart she talked about and would pick up offense easily. Even the way someone said something to me or neglected to say something would hurt me and put me on the attack. I also had a critical heart. I was always on my mom's case about storing junk in her house rather than cleaning it out. Needless to say, I began to realize I had my own "stockpile of junk", most of which was in my heart!

As far back as I could remember my prayer had been "Lord, help me to implement Proverbs 31:10 in my life". I wanted the entire Proverbs 31 woman in me but that was going to take a long time. Proverbs 31:10 says 'if you can find a truly good wife, she is worth more than precious gems'! I certainly wasn't the precious gem yet; I was more in the charcoal stage with an unformed diamond inside. God showed me that I needed a spiritual heart transplant in order to become a Proverbs 31 woman. Unforgiveness was a part of my negative heart condition and the root of many needed house repairs. My unforgiving heart went way back to some unhealthy seeds planted into me a long time ago. I knew of no one better to go to for that open-heart surgery than the Lord. He was the best heart surgeon I knew and I didn't even have to get on a waiting list to see Him. All the king's horses and all the king's men could not put Mr. Humpty Dumpty back together again, but God could and would put me back together again and better than I was before.

All My Life I Wanted My Dad's Approval

My daddy was a wonderful man and I don't want to discount the good things he did for people. To get to the root of some my unhealthy fruit I had to look back where the unhealthy seeds came from.
Unfortunately, my daddy was raised with a lot of rejection and physical abuse. Even though he was the first man I ever knew that would go the

extra mile for people in need, he really hurt my mother, and sometimes me, emotionally throughout the years. Without even realizing it, I had stored up a lot of this hurt while I was growing up.

As with most things, my feelings of rejection had small beginnings that turned into bigger hurts, starting with my daddy wanting a boy with all his heart and me being a girl instead. My mother didn't know if she could oblige my dad in producing the boy he wanted so she prayed to cover both bases. She asked the Lord to please let me look just like my daddy whether I was a boy or girl. God heard my mother's prayers and obliged her and out I came looking just like my dad. Mother laughed about it for years but I could tell that she also felt hurt and disappointment over the fact that daddy was working late on the night of my birth and didn't show up until after I was born.

From these early seeds of not being what my daddy's heart desired, I hungered for his love and approval. I wanted my dad to be proud of me and to tell me how proud he was of me. Instead, he would often use harsh words to put my mother or me down. Jokes of how fat mother was and how careless and stupid I was were words that were planted deep into my heart. By the time I was grown, I was determined to find me a man who would love me no matter what. I didn't want to be second or third best. And I certainly did not want to be called by some other woman's name, the way my father did to my mom. I wanted my husband blind but not in a physical sense, just to the desire to ever want to look at any other woman. Remember the fairy tale? With that in mind, I came into our marriage with a lot of misguided expectations.

That Man Loved To Work, Just Like My Dad

For most of our married life, Arnold's love was his work. Instead of being married to an alcoholic, I was married to a work-aholic. I heard a pastor at a Bible study share that the Lord had convicted him that he had been having an affair. "What are You talking about?" was his response to the Lord. The Lord answered "You're having an affair with your job. It's more important to you than your wife". The man was convicted by the Holy Spirit and repented. I wanted Arnold to be convicted about this too and couldn't wait to get home and tell him this great story so he could get his life right, just like this pastor did. But it didn't happen that way and the words I shared seemed to fall on deaf ears. All I got for that great story was more hurt because Arnold was blind and wouldn't see! Oh, why wouldn't he listen to me? I just knew that if he would listen to me, he would see! With feelings of resentment and unforgiveness being added to the already slow burning fire in my heart, I was deceived into thinking that the best value in the world was being accepted by the men in my life. Since I wasn't, then there wasn't much value to me!

Welcome Enemy, Come On In!

As the years rolled by, I continued to store up all the hurts I had accumulated during our marriage until the granddaddy of them all occurred. I became very hurt by something that Arnold had done and in carrying this offense, I opened the door to the enemy once more. I planned a party for Arnold's 65th birthday. On the big day, I worked very hard preparing a special birthday luncheon for him. When he came home, he seemed to enjoy the lunch and the people who were there but he didn't really show very much excitement about it. I didn't think much of his lack of response since I tend to get excited about things and show my feelings, and Arnold doesn't. I just chalked it up to our being different. That night while I was getting ready to go out to eat, our daughter Rebecca called from Florida to wish Arnold a happy birthday. I overheard Arnold share something that they had done for him at work and the excitement of it and how funny it was. No mention of "yours truly" and the work done for his special birthday lunch, though. I won't even mention what they did to surprise him at work but what started out as a woman coming in for a job interview soon turned into a woman in a birthday suit! Arnold thought it was very funny but it had me fuming. How in the world could this possibly have been funny to my man? I thought "after all, this man is a Christian, not some lost sinner". I wasn't seeing any humor in the birthday cake he brought home from work, either. This birthday cake was shaped and decorated as a naked woman!

By the time Arnold got off the phone, my anger had heated up from a simmer to a full-fledged kitchen fire! Our dinner plans suddenly changed. "What's the matter?" was Arnold's question to me. For the first two or three "nothing's", I kept my cool but finally the wind blew. At first it was just a small cyclone and the Holy Spirit surely must have gotten out of my way because His ways were nowhere in sight! This voluptuous cake that had been made in the shape of a woman with a 42DD chest had now been turned into one sized at 34A. I was surprised at how simple it was for me to do this breast reduction – and without any formal training, either!

For two weeks I cleaned up pink and flesh colored icing from my walls, ceiling, and all sorts of places in the kitchen. We were a very miserable couple for a while. I tried so hard to make Arnold understand how much he had hurt me, not realizing the offense I had received had opened the door for the enemy to have a field day. He was kicking field goals all over the place and I was the ball holder! One night Arnold and I went to our Bible study and my heart was in torment. We sat there and proceeded as usual until finally the wind began to blow and I began to share my feelings. Our friends refereed and God began to use them as they shared how **I had let the enemy in.** Hey, aren't friends supposed to be on the wife's side?! I just knew they'd be on Arnold's case and see how horrible he was to have even wanted to look at a naked woman other than me (real or sculpted from cake and icing). But all they could see was how "yours truly" responded and that I had opened the door to the enemy in my reaction to what had taken place. I thought I was more like Jesus in over turning the moneychanger's table. But if my friends love me, they won't always tell me what I want to hear. They'll tell me what I need to hear in order to make things better. They prayed for us that night and God began to repair our broken down walls. God spoke to me that night that it didn't matter so much what Arnold did or didn't do; it was my response to Arnold that opened a door to the enemy. At the start of this birthday celebration, I had reacted full of hurt and pain. As this festered, it hardened into pride, self-righteousness, and condemnation. God wanted me to release Arnold to Him and let Him deal with Arnold and his birthday celebration. I was to forgive Arnold and be free!

More and more I was beginning to see that when I try to change others, I never get very far. I wanted my husband to be as disgusted with what he saw in the cake and what had happened at his office as I was, but he wasn't. The resentment and resulting bitterness inside me was letting the enemy have a field day and God wanted me to be strong and not let what was happening destroy me. I had not passed the test! I remember an old TV show that we used to watch called "The Love Boat". On a particular episode the cruise director, Julie, was going through all sorts of tests in order to receive a promotion. When she finished her test, she reported to the Captain with a look of confidence. It was as if she could already hear "well done, my good and faithful servant"! But much to her surprise, the Captain said that he was sorry but that she hadn't passed the tests. Julie did not come unglued or reply with sarcasm and bitterness; she stayed poised and confident, thanking the Captain as if she understood and proceeded to walk out. As her hand reached for the door, the Captain spoke up again and said she had just passed the test. **Her response to her rejection and her failure had been the final test.** I felt like God was showing me something. My responses to hurtful things were not like Julie's response in the Love Boat. My reactions to the events and people in my life needed to change or this boat was going to sink.

They're Everywhere! They're Everywhere!

One night I had a dream in which there were worms all over the kitchen. It seemed pretty gross but then sin usually is. I put something on them and killed most of them. Then Arnold and I went out of town but when we came back, they had grown all over the faucet and in the sink and other places. They were everywhere and I couldn't seem to get rid of them!

The next morning before I even began to pray, I knew immediately that the word wormwood (bitter) and worms were God's way of telling me there was some ugly fruit in someone's life. I didn't want to be kept out of the "promise land" any longer than I had to. I asked the Lord to give me the revelation and interpretation from the dream and show me what He was trying to reveal to my heart. After just a few minutes, this thought came to mind. "There are many kitchens where bitterness and resentment have taken place, wounds from wives to husbands and vise versa". Oh, how true that was; many times, I held Arnold captive by the resentment and bitterness in my heart. I also knew there were plenty of times where he had resentment towards me, right there at our kitchen table! I began to pray about the resentment that had been hardening my heart into wormwood:

> **"I curse this root of bitterness that is in my heart, Lord, and I thank You for a new forgiving heart. I ask that You heal any bitter memory I have in my heart and I pray that my heart would be cleansed. I pray for my heart to be healed and for deliverance by the power of the Holy Spirit. Let love find its way into my heart. Love hardly notices when others would do it wrong. (Psalm 147:3 & 1 Corinthians 13:4) Holy Spirit bring me love, love, love!"**

Another Fox in the Hen House

Another test, another fox! God wanted to be sure I learned this lesson. One night while I was helping a friend set up for a meeting, I thought about asking him to pray for my mother. Since I had prayed for his ministry and blessed him many times, I thought why not ask him to pray for mine, too. I hesitated because he was such a busy man. After a second time of this coming to my mind, I decided to go for it and ask him to pray for my mother. I could feel the Holy Spirit moving on me as I shared with him about my mother and the needs she had. He smiled and said "we'll pray for her tonight; there will be lots of people here and we can all pray for her." I knew in that moment why I was supposed to listen to God and the still, small voice of the Spirit. There would be other leaders there that night and some mighty prayer warriors, too. My sweet mama was about to be prayed for by all of them; she deserved it after all she had done for other people.

That night the people came and the people went with no mention of praying for mother. When most of them had left, the thought came to go and ask him again. I really didn't want to ask him again; after all, I had already asked him one time and he didn't do it. But God said to humble myself so I walked up to him again with the same request to pray for my mother. Surprise and a look of embarrassment came on his face as he shared that he had forgotten but there were still many people there who could pray for her. My daughter, Rebecca and I waited a bit and then started gathering the last few things together to walk out the door. This time when I walked passed him, I decided not to mention my mother again. There would be no other promptings from the Holy Spirit to have him pray for her. A little fox, named Resentment, had just snuck into my hen house.

I was very hurt and disappointed. How could this man, this Christian friend, have forgotten to pray over my important request, especially after I had spent many hours and a lot of energy helping him? It was late when we got home and upon entering the house, the phone rang. It seemed that while he was driving home, the Holy Spirit had brought to mind that, once again, he had forgotten about my prayer request for my mother. We prayed over the phone but the hurt and the offense went so deep that it took a long time to get over it. The more I dwelled on it, the more negative things I thought about this person; I began to create a mental score card on him that recorded all the wrong things he had done. That night had been just one more offense to add to all the others I had with him and I went to bed very hurt and wounded. As the resentment continued to grow, I unknowingly allowed the enemy to steal my "eggs" of peace, joy, and love.

After I got over the initial hurt and disappointment, the Lord brought to my mind "You are to pray for him". Ouch! Pray for him? I don't want to pray for him; he was supposed to pray about my request! My focus was on this man and what he had done or not done for me and it was tormenting me. My focus was obviously wrong. First, I had to repent of the pride that did not want or let me forgive him. Again, I was reminded by the still small voice of the Holy Spirit of all the times I had hurt my daughter, or my son or one of my friends. I'm sure I wasn't even aware of some of the times when I would hurt someone. He was reminding me of my past mistakes, but for a good reason -- to learn from them. The Lord wanted me to be more understanding because there had been times when I was insensitive to the needs of others in my life, as well. I had been focused on self, self, and more self! This would be a lesson that would help me to give more compassion and forgiveness to others.

A Moment of Truth

Up until now, my thought life consisted of: "When were people going to treat me the way I think I should be treated?" Obviously, I was missing the point. The point of truth that God wanted me to see and live was that I was to love others, no matter what! I began to pray and cry out to God to reshape my life. The Lord tells us to strip off every weight that slows us down (Hebrews 12:1). I wouldn't mind shedding about ten pounds or so but the Lord was talking about a different kind of weight. He wanted me to shed the excess baggage I carried around in the form of hurt, bitterness, and resentment. The Holy Spirit made me aware of the unforgiveness, one poisoned root at a time. He started reshaping my life and showing me that I had problems of which I was not even aware. My chains of unforgiveness and bitterness were robbing me of peace and joy. God would show me that it would choke the life out of me just like the vine of kudzu chokes the life out of a tree. Many times, I could forgive quite easily; I found I could just renounce it, cut its ugly head off and never see another piece of unhealthy fruit from that tree again. But it wasn't always like that; forgiving someone could sometimes take me a few days, weeks, months or longer. Each time the memory of what had happened or what was said re-surfaced, I would have to get out the weed kill and spray the same weeds again and again. Obviously, my weed kill wasn't very effective!

The Lord began to deal with me concerning my perception of unforgiveness. He showed me that I wasn't discerning the ways of the enemy and the enemy was robbing me through these offenses. I didn't understand that the enemy was trying to destroy me through what others said or did to me. The enemy was definitely pulling the string on my yoyo and each time there was an offense, I would go up and down. I began to pray, asking the Lord why I wasn't taking out the enemy like Gideon did. The enemy greatly outnumbered Gideon and yet when he followed God's plan he defeated the enemy with only a few good men! "Why am I not doing this Lord? Why am I always hurt?" was my prayer. The Holy Spirit gave me my answer, "Because of the unforgiveness"! I hadn't been following God's plan; He told me to forgive. I continued to pray: "Lord why am I unable to forgive someone, especially when I know that I've needed forgiveness for the times I've blown it?" The thought that came to mind was this -- pride! **"Humility enables you to forgive, but pride won't let you."** Someone once said that the Messiah's strength is shown by humility where Satan's strength is revealed through pride. I began to renounce pride from my life and asked the Lord to place upon me a Colossians 3:12 coat of humility. 'Wanda, clothe yourself wherever you go with compassion, kindness, humility, gentleness, and patience!'

Slam Dunk The Enemy

Mordecai Ham, a great man of God, said we should never enter into battle without knowing the nature of the foe. I was aware of some of the enemy's tactics but, obviously, not enough. God wanted to warn me and let me see where I was blind. He wanted me to know the tactics of the enemy concerning unforgiveness. God's Word would strike the enemy and defeat him if I would use it just like Jesus did in the wilderness. Jesus didn't let what the enemy said unglue him; He unglued the enemy! I was praying more and more and asking God for insight and revelation on how to stop the enemy from stealing through unforgiveness. How am I going to slam-dunk the enemy? By forgiving others no matter what they have done. If Satan is going to try to rob me, then I have to learn to stand and truly know what the Word says. It is one thing to speak the Word and it is another thing to walk it out. I slam dunk the enemy and walk on the water when I don't turn and look back. I slam-dunk him when I say no more! I slam-dunk him when I refuse to dwell on a bad thought! I slam dunk him when I let go of what I did in the past or what someone did to me. **I will not keep a scorecard!** The enemy's plans are destroyed when I ask God to search my heart, shine His light into it, and let me see what's really inside of me. "God deliver me from all my focus on other's faults and what they've done to me!" Forgiveness slam-dunks the enemy, big time; praising the Lord cuts his head off, too! The enemy has no power over me when I'm focused on God and not on what's happened to me. As a dear friend's husband once said, "Life is not about me; life is about Jesus". I'm slam-dunking the enemy when I can realize as someone once said "It doesn't matter what others do to me in the light of what God and Jesus have done for me!" Forgiveness bleeds all over the enemy's plans every time. Just one drop of Jesus' blood is enough to defeat the enemy if I will only forgive.

Walking the Talk

I have learned that offenses will always be lurking at every corner because the enemy does not want to give up; he wants me to give up. I listened as Arnold read from an account in the newspaper of a woman that was robbed in broad daylight at a local mall. As I sat at the table with Arnold, I began to pray that the theft be stopped in our city. God began to give me His perspective and show me how offenses, misunderstandings, and bitterness rob us, even in broad daylight! Without forgiveness, I am like an open cash register drawer; any and all can take what they want. A storeowner uses every precaution (security systems, locked cash registers, safes, etc.) to protect his store, money, and merchandise; so why shouldn't I try to protect myself and family from being robbed by Satan through unforgiveness?!

The Word says Satan destroys and he loves to create misunderstandings, even on small, everyday type of events. One of those times came when our son Franklin called to say he was sick with a sore throat and asked if we had any lemons. I remembered my mother's lemon and honey remedy for colds and all the lemons I had in the refrigerator. I told Arnold I was going to run some lemons over to Franklin. Arnold responded that he wanted to make sure we had enough for us and not to take all of them. I was stunned; how could Arnold think of himself when Franklin was the sick one, especially when Arnold didn't even like lemons?! Satan used what could have been a totally innocent response from Arnold to create a spark of anger and resentment within me. I perceived this as Arnold being selfish and more concerned with himself than with our sick son. By the time I walked out of the house, I could feel the offense starting to rise up in me. I soon recognized that this was a tactic of the enemy and that he almost had me right where he wanted– in the palm of his hand. He wanted me to open the door to this offense so he could have permission to squash me. With that thought in mind, I stopped right on that top step of my porch as I sensed the Holy Spirit leading me to pray and said out loud, "I refuse this offense!" In that moment, the offense left and I felt the cool refreshing peace of the Holy Spirit coming all over me, erasing what the enemy had just tried to do. A sense of God's presence started to fill me and my joy was returning by the time I got to the car. Remember the song "Born Free"? That's the way I want to be, free from the grasp of the enemy!

Another temptation to take offense occurred a couple of days later. I had stopped by the grocery store to pick up a few things. While I was waiting for the clerk to ring-up my order, a man came up and put his things down on the conveyor belt in front of me. The sales clerk stopped waiting on me and began to ring up the man's merchandise. The cashier asked the man if he wanted to use his debit card and all I could think of was "what did he just do"? Again the voice became louder in my mind, **"EXCUSE ME! Did that man just break in front of me?!!"** I was shocked and dumbfounded to say the least that this man just blatantly cut in front of me without even speaking. Then I heard another voice. It seems that the Holy Spirit was there with me, too. "Do not receive this offense". I struggled with my pride for just a moment but then prayed for that coat of humility and let it go.

When Does Healing Come?

The thought continued to come to mind about praying for the healing of my own wounded heart. I did not quite understand what this meant. I asked the Lord to show me and to bring these things out of the darkness of my heart. Sometimes the wounds inflicted by the enemy can need just as much healing and reconstructive surgery to the heart as the wounds inflicted by a knife or gun. One day the thought came, "forgive your daddy for what he did to you and to your mother". I thought I had forgiven him but every time I thought about him I still felt pain. Most of these memories were painful ones where he had hurt my mother. I soon realized I was carrying the offense of another; I was holding on to unforgiveness over what had been done to someone I cared for. Now I was being held captive by carrying this offense. I prayed and forgave my daddy for every time he hurt my mother or me. When does healing come? **It comes when I <u>choose</u> to forgive.** How do I get there? By being willing to die to self and what I want or what was done to me and to choose what God wants for me instead. This means dying to me! This means dying to pride and my wanting revenge. The Lord says all vengeance is His! (Deut 32:35 and Romans 12:19) This means I'm trusting God that one day there will be justice even if I don't live to see it. God says that if I hold anything against anyone, forgive him, so that my Father in heaven may forgive me of my sins (Matthew 6:14). I can forgive with the help of the Lord, even if someone who has hurt me or one of my loved ones never changes. It's not what was done to me that destroyed me as much as it was my holding on to the offense. **My beholding the problem, rather than the Lamb** was what gave the enemy the upper hand and showed my lack of trust in the Lord to handle things for me. Proverbs 16:6 was one of those lighthouses that helped my ship to come in. It says 'sin is atoned for by mercy and by truth and by the fear of the Lord one keeps away from evil.' I'm accountable to Him, not to the ones that have hurt me. Now when I have memories of my daddy, it's something good. It doesn't mean I think he's a saint now; I just know I've forgiven him and the thoughts of him are not rooted in pain anymore. I can remember the good times and there were plenty of them! Emotional healing was the fruit of forgiving my daddy.

Matthew 9:2 says "Some men brought him a paralyzed boy on a mat. When Jesus saw their faith, He said to the sick boy 'Cheer up son; for I have FORGIVEN your sins'". I became aware that it is much more important to concentrate on God's forgiveness and His healing of the spiritual sickness that was in me than to concentrate on God's power to heal any physical sickness I might have. Malachi 4:2 told me something, too. 'For those who fear My Name, the Son of Righteousness will rise with healing in His wings. And you will go free leaping with joy like a calf let out into the pasture'. When I fear the name of the Lord, I care more about what He says than what anyone else says or does to me. I can trust Him and He will rise with healing in His wings and abolish the plans of the enemy!
God was certainly working on me, changing me, and giving me more sensitivity to His voice and to His ways. God also brought another scripture to mind with a story I could relate to. Mark 5:2-5 talks about a man who needed help. This man was so strong that he would just snap the chains from his wrists and smash the shackles on his feet. All day long, he would scream and cut himself with stones. When I read this scripture, God spoke to my heart that this is what I do to myself when I don't forgive. I am constantly in torment and cutting myself

repeatedly with sharp rocks where I am already wounded. God wanted me to remember His forgiveness. He wanted me to remember where He had poured out His love and mercy and forgiven me and healed me. Deuteronomy 30:6 was another freeing truth. 'The Lord, your God, will cleanse your heart, Wanda, and the hearts of all your descendents so that you will love Him with all your heart and soul and so you may live'. "Lord", I prayed, "cleanse my heart so that I might really be able to love those who are not even nice to me". Unless I am willing to forfeit my rights to hang onto the hurt and forgive, I will not live and love will not find a way. Jesus forgave no matter what was done to him. **When I forgive, I am healed!**

The following was part of my prayer for forgiveness:

"Father, in the name of Jesus, I make this decision. I forgive myself. I am not condemned; I am a child of God. I am born again. I am washed in the blood of Jesus and I am whole and righteous because of the Lamb of God. Forgive me for every root of bitterness that has taken place in my heart. I now take an axe and sever it; it has no place in me. Bitterness is of Satan; Wrath is of Satan; I reject it. I renounce it and I repent of it. I receive healing in my mind; in my body and in my spirit. I will not walk in condemnation.

Father, I pray, in Jesus' name, that You will reveal to me anyone I am not forgiving. I renounce all pride from my life that would keep me from forgiving them. I ask that You place upon me Your coat of Humility! I also ask You to remind me as often as I need it how many times You have forgiven me and let love have its way in me. I pray that I would be released from all hurt and all the pains that anyone has ever caused me. I ask You, Holy Spirit, to come with Your love and shed abroad that perfect love in my heart. I choose to forgive my father, my mother, my husband, my family, my friends, myself or anyone else who has hurt me or disappointed me. I release them from all my expectations and disappointments. I forgive all of those who have set themselves against me, even from the day of my birth. Forgive me, Father, from looking to any other person outside of You for the love I need, Your love for me that can only come from Your son, Jesus. Free me, Lord, from judging my husband or anyone else. Forgive me for the resentment in my heart. I know You have heard my prayer and I believe You are setting me free!

Lord, I want my focus to be off of me and what was done to me. I want my mind set on things above and not below. I make this decision: no one can offend me. I will not be offended. To be offended is contrary to the will of God. I will bless those who curse me and I will bless those who use me. I ask You to look upon me as one who desires to love You with all of my heart and all of my soul. I command everything that is within me to bless the Lord, to sing praises, to have joy, to receive strength, wisdom, knowledge, understanding, and patience. Bless me now, Lord, and may I be a blessing to You, as well as others. I thank You for Your help, Holy Spirit, in accomplishing all of this, in Jesus' name. Amen."

Scripture Used In This Chapter

Proverbs 31:10 Who can find a virtuous and capable wife? She is worth more than precious rubies.

Psalm 147:3 He heals the brokenhearted, binding up their wounds.

1 Corinthians 13:4 Love is patient and kind. Love is not jealous or boastful or proud

Hebrews 12:1 Therefore, since we are surrounded by such a huge crowd of witnesses to the life of faith, let us strip off every weight that slows us down, especially the sin that so easily hinders our progress. And let us run with endurance the race that God has set before us.

Colossians 3:12 Since God chose you to be the holy people whom he loves, you must clothe yourselves with tenderhearted mercy, kindness, humility, gentleness, and patience.

Deuteronomy 32:35 I will take vengeance; I will repay those who deserve it. In due time their feet will slip. Their day of disaster will arrive, and their destiny will overtake them.

Romans 12:19 Dear friends, never avenge yourselves. Leave that to God. For it is written, "I will take vengeance; I will repay those who deserve it," says the Lord.

Matthew 6:14 If you forgive those who sin against you, your heavenly Father will forgive you.

Proverbs 16:6 Unfailing love and faithfulness cover sin; evil is avoided by fear of the LORD.

Matthew 9:2 Some people brought to him a paralyzed man on a mat. Seeing their faith, Jesus said to the paralyzed man, "Take heart, son! Your sins are forgiven."

Malachi 4:2 But for you who fear my name, the Sun of Righteousness will rise with healing in his wings. And you will go free, leaping with joy like calves let out to pasture.

Mark 5:2-5 Just as Jesus was climbing from the boat, a man possessed by an evil spirit ran out from a cemetery to meet him. This man lived among the tombs and could not be restrained, even with a chain.

Whenever he was put into chains and shackles--as he often was--he snapped the chains from his wrists and smashed the shackles. No one was strong enough to control him. All day long and throughout the night, he would wander among the tombs and in the hills, screaming and hitting himself with stones.

Deuteronomy 30:6 The LORD your God will cleanse your heart and the hearts of all your descendants so that you will love him with all your heart and soul, and so you may live!

A HEALING BREEZE

The Great Physician!

First, I would like to say I am hardly ever sick. And second, I never knew anyone could be healed of anything unless he or she first went to the doctor and got some medicine. I was having some sporadic physical problems but had not yet thought things were dire enough to warrant a doctor visit. Arnold and I began to plan a weekend trip to Atlanta; we were looking forward to attending a church in Atlanta we had heard a lot about. I had not been experiencing any problems when we left to go to Atlanta but as we dressed for church on Sunday morning, I began to feel sick. All I could think about was the disappointment of not getting to go to this church I had heard so much about. I asked Arnold to go to the service without me and to bring back a tape of the service so I could listen to it later. When Arnold returned from church, he shared that the pastor had not preached that day but that they had a guest speaker. I was disappointed; not only was the speaker different than I had hoped but the message he had was different, too. The pastor, Mark Rutland, shared that God had spoken to his heart that the message was to be different than the one originally planned. Pastor Rutland said he had been cruising down the rivers of Peru with alligators all around, asking God when he would get to be on the platform to preach. When would God use him? God spoke to his heart that he was exactly where he needed to be and if God couldn't use him with the alligators out there then He would never be able to use him on any other platform. Good message, but to be honest, as I listened to the taped sermon, I really didn't think the message was for me. I thought about our pastor who was facing some difficulties and just knew before we even finished listening to the tape that this message was for him.

Upon our return home, I proceeded to feel much better and all thoughts of going to a doctor completely left me. I gave the tape to our pastor and told him to listen to it as soon as he could and get it back to me. He gave it to me a few days later and didn't seem impressed with it at all. Then I thought of a friend. She was having a lot of marital problems and surely, this was for her. I shared it with her and proceeded to forget about it. A few days later my physical problems came back and even worse than before. Reluctantly, I decided I'd better use some wisdom and went to the doctor. Several days after the examination, the doctor wanted to see both Arnold and me. The doctor found a lump in my breast and my pap smear had returned with a bad report. I thought I would fall apart right then and there, sitting across the desk from the doctor. Immediately, I called several friends who began to pray for me. The friend that I had given the tape to earlier called before the day was over and said "Wanda, the tape is actually for you. I'm going to bring it back to you and let you hear it one more time." She was right. When I went back and re-listened, my name was all over it. I had asked the Lord many, many times "when would He use me?"! I seemed to be in the same situation as Pastor Rutland, headed down the river in a rocky canoe with alligators everywhere. Only my gators were a bad pap smear and a lump in my breast. Where was my faith? I'm sorry to say it seemed that it went right out of the boat and down to the bottom of the river.

For the first time in my life, a part of the bible I had never seen before leaped off the page and came straight into my heart. James 5:14 'Are any among you sick? (Yes I was!) Then they should call for the elders of the church and have them pray over them, anointing them with oil in the name of the Lord.' That's exactly what I did. I don't remember if I had the oil treatment or not but I did go forward and the leaders in the church did lay hands on me and pray for me. I decided that if God said this was a way to be healed, then I would believe Him and just stand on His word.

The next couple of weeks were horrible. I was so self absorbed that all I could think about was leaving this world and Arnold getting a new woman, probably in record time. He might give me a few weeks to cool off. But who would the kids get to take care of them? All of these wonderful, Godly thoughts were racing through my mind. Finally, one day as I sat at the kitchen table I thought about my faith or lack of it. I thought about how I had told the Lord, just months before, that no matter what he asked me to do I would serve him. And now here I was falling apart when my alligators showed up. That day as I sat there, I repented! I repented for my lack of faith. I repented because I had said I would serve God no matter what. I repented because I was so fearful; I asked the Lord to forgive me and I asked Him to deliver me from all self- pity and self-focus. I was not helping God one bit if all I could do was to think about me. Then I found myself saying "God if I have only six weeks or six months left on this earth I want to spend them serving You. Would You please take my mind off of myself and put it on someone else who I could bless?"

James 5:16 says "Confess your sins to each other and pray for each other so that you may be healed." In that moment, I had confessed my sins to God. The next thing that happened was the rest of the scripture. When I went to bed that night, I was determined (with the help of God, of course) that I wouldn't lie there and pray about me. I remember saying "Lord, who do You want me to pray for? Lord, who needs Your help right now?" There were many people who could have fit this prayer request but God gave me the one He wanted me to reach out to. My mother's neighbor was dying and didn't know the Lord. I found myself crying out to God on his behalf, praying that he would come to know the Lord before he left this world. I had no sooner gotten these words out of my mouth then something went all over me. I felt a tingling sensation from my head all the way down to my feet. I wondered, "What in the world was that?" I had no idea and just put it out of my mind and drifted off to sleep.

When I went in for my surgery, they took a little bit longer than they had planned and when the doctor came out he explained why. He said when he made the first incision into the breast he found no lump. He then decided to make another incision, cutting in the opposite direction but again found no lump. He said rather than go in and cut straight down and have to remove any more of the breast tissue, he decided to leave well enough alone. And when they got the test results back from another procedure concerning the bad pap smear, there was nothing wrong there either. God had healed me! The night I experienced the tingling sensation was when the second part of James 5:16 became true for me.

I learned many things that day. God can use doctors to heal and He can use His supernatural powers. I also realized that I had not asked God to heal me. I had had hands laid on me at the church just as God's Word says and I had repented and been asking him to save my mother's neighbor. But I was alone when God healed me. Taking my eyes off myself, putting them on someone else, and confessing my sins had all proved to be fruitful! God had done so much for me! "He heals my broken heart, binding up my wounds (Psalms 147:3). You must serve only the LORD your God. If you do, I will bless you with food and water, and I will keep you healthy" (Exodus 23:25). I had confessed my sins and He had taken sickness away from me (James 5:16)! But I trust in You, O Lord; I say You are my God. My times are in Your hands; deliver me from my enemies and from those who pursue me. Let Your face shine on your servant; save me in Your unfailing love. Be strong, Wanda, and take heart all of you who put your trust in the Lord" (Psalms 31:14-16&24).

He Leads Me Beside The Cool Still Waters And Oh, Does He Restore My Soul!!!

Some years later, I was working for a cookie company as a public relations person, soliciting some business for Christmas. After a few days of pains in my stomach that seemed to be getting worse, I decided maybe it was time for me to take some action. I took some over-the-counter medicine for a few days but did not get any better. Each time I would go to work, I began to hurt so bad that I would think I couldn't make it home. Thinking I just needed to take it easy for a while, I took a few days off from work. But when I went back to work, I would cringe with pain. Finally, one morning I told Arnold about my problem and asked him if he would go and get me some more medicine. Surely, this would do the trick this time. It failed to work, so Arnold called the doctor's office. I was given a prescription for some medicine and told that if I was not better in 24 hours to go to the hospital. Within twelve hours, I was on the bathroom floor in agony. Arnold took me to the hospital, where they admitted me and began to run tests. As I lay on the stretcher in the emergency room, one of the thoughts I had was that my time must be up! Other thoughts followed this one, "Who's going to do the prayer retreat that I was planning?" "The enemy is out to destroy me!" I believed this was an attack from Satan to steal and destroy my life; what he didn't bargain for were the prayers that were doing battle in saving my life.

While I was in the emergency room, one of the doctors had asked me if there was any particular doctor that I would like to call. With no one coming to mind, I can remember saying, "just make sure he's a godly man" and with that he smiled and left. God answered that prayer for me and while I lay in the emergency room, a Doctor Parker walked around the curtain. I could see God in that man and my heart leaped that He had answered my prayers so quickly. Within a few hours, I knew I was in big trouble. After my x-ray, I was given the grim news that they would be on the alert for the possibility of surgery before morning. I was told I might need a colostomy; my colon had torn, my fever was high and my white blood count had gone through the roof! Infection was all in my body. I was given four or five shots of morphine that night with little relief from the intense pain. I was told that I couldn't be given anymore because they had to keep track of where and to what degree I was hurting. But I was grateful, even for the little help.

Arnold phoned several people that night, some even came to the hospital. Seeing my daughter-in-law, Jenny, and our son, Franklin,

Rebecca wants everyone to know how much God loves them. She has learned that the only way you can limit God is with your mind. Her Step-dad Arnold told her to always dream big. She wants to share those same encouraging words with others. Come to God with your hearts desire, and expect the impossible. She says there is so much out there waiting for you and it is amazing what can happen if only you'll believe!

Rebecca with one of her favorite people, her sister in law Jennifer.

Arnold and I took a fun filled ride down the beach with our grand-dog Fletcher and his dad Franklin close by

Maligne Lake was just one of the many beautiful spots Arnold and I saw while we were in Canada.

standing there in his police uniform was a very welcome sight. I remember Jennifer calling her Mom and Dad, asking them to pray, and hearing her respond to their obvious question of whether or not they need to come. "Yes, Mom, I think you'd better!" That night was a nightmare of pain and by the next morning, Arnold was on the phone calling more people to pray; this time he called the church office. I can still hear him say "Mary, Wanda's in the hospital and needs prayer". I knew that Mary Rogers would pray and was excited at the prospects of Mary praying for me even while I was lying there in pain. Mary told me later that she never works at the church in the morning but that day she did! That day God had Mary there for me! By that afternoon, our daughter-in-law, Jenny, had called her Dad in Mobile. He got on his computer immediately, giving out information of my needs over the Internet, all the way to New Mexico. Arnold called our daughter, Rebecca, in Orlando and I found out later that she also began making calls in the wee hours of the night. Thank God for people who will pray even when it's still dark outside! There are those that prayed for me that I might never know their names until I get to heaven, but I thank them! When someone asks me to pray for them, it becomes one of the biggest things on my agenda. I don't put it off; it could be a matter of life and death. I honestly have to say there were times while I lay there praying and others were praying for me that I wondered, "Where is God"? Things seemed like such a whirlwind that night, I couldn't believe the storm that was blowing and trying to destroy my whole life, all for the sake of two chocolate brownies! I had eaten some of those same brownies a few months back and had had a similar problem but on a much smaller scale. At that time, Arnold had prayed for me and I was immediately better! Not this time. What the apple did for Eve, the brownie was doing for me. I had eaten the forbidden fruit and I was almost out of here!

Right off, I was told that I would be in the hospital for four or five days. This, in itself, sent up an alarm because no one stays in the hospital that long in this day and age. I only stayed in the hospital for two and half days when I had my hysterectomy, so this must mean big trouble. I was finally moved to a room and preceded at a very fast rate to recuperate. While I was being restored in my hospital room, the thought came to my mind to ask Arnold to bring my tape player and a particular song. It was a song called, "There's Healing in This Place". I remember playing this tape over and over at a prayer retreat and watching God minister mightily. Reasoning was sure taking its toll on my life because the first thing I began to question and think about was not to ask Arnold to bring the tape. He had brought several things to me already and for him to wait on me and do for me was a new thing; I was used to taking care of him! Then the thought came about the ministry that tape would be to the nurses that would come by. Again, I began to reason: "My time in the hospital would be so short and the nurses certainly would not have time to come by and listen to a song." The thought of this song continued to come, so I finally gave in on the 11th hour, right before Arnold came back to the hospital. I decided to kick my reasoning out the door and listen to that still small voice. That night Arnold left me with my tape player and special song!

When I began to play the tape, one of the nurses came into the room. She was so touched by the song that she stayed and listened to it. Before the morning was over, nurses from other floors were coming in and being touched by God through this tape. That Sunday morning one nurse came in and told me she had run into another nurse who told her "you have to go by that room; there's such an anointing there. You just have to hear that song!" The nurse told me that she really didn't have time to come by my room that morning; she was about to get off from work and go to church to teach a Sunday school class. But when she got on the elevator and began to punch the down button, she found herself punching the button to come up to my room. The Spirit of the Lord took hold of that woman as tears flowed in the presence of God in that room that morning; she met with Him before church!

The next morning Dr. Parker came by to check on me and stood in amazement at the drop in the fever, the drop in the white blood count, and at the change in me. All he could do was shake his head and say "I missed it". He thought he must have made the wrong diagnosis because of my remarkable recovery. I remember sitting there and telling this fine man of God that he had not missed it at all; God had been healing me and people everywhere were praying. Dr Parker came back later with several doctors, to find me sitting in a chair as if I was a visitor. One of the new doctors had looked over at me and kind of nodded when he came in and then looked over at the empty bed. Dr. Parker told him that I was the patient and with that, he smiled. The new doctor looked amazed! I told every one that God was healing me. I'm not sure what the new doctor's thought, but I knew that Dr. Parker knew who was in charge of my healing!

On my third day in the hospital, I couldn't wait to get the needle that was feeding me out of my veins. Up until that time all I had had was the liquid through the tube and needle; not even a drop of water could be given to me. They had to make sure that I wasn't going to have to be rushed to surgery. I can remember lying there and thinking "on the third day Jesus rose up!" A lot happened on that third day for him, so why not for me? I was drinking though, but from a well that no man could see and I was getting plenty of living water. I found myself believing that I was going to get that needle out that day and as I was envisioning them removing my needle, I noticed that my arm was swollen. In fact, it was much larger than the other arm. Wow this was "proof in the pudding"; the needle was going to have to come out and this arm was to get a rest. I called for the nurse to come in and she immediately took the needle out. Boy, oh boy, my vision was not in vain. When the doctor came in, I shared with him this wonderful idea of no needle. I hoped to receive mercy from him but he proceeded to pronounce a sentence of needle and tube feeding for another day or two.

The nurse came in to hook me back up to my needle and bag. I was very sure I wouldn't need it but a little reluctant to get up out of the bed and make a run for it. She proceeded to find a new vein to put the needle in; after many tries, she finally found one. Right before she stuck me, I began to pray out loud. I guess she thought I was talking to her because she asked me "what did you say?" I told her I was praying and with that, she put the needle in and immediately a huge knot-came up, the size of a small golf ball. The vein had blown up. This couldn't be happening and after praying, too! The nurse felt so bad and apologized and I said, "Let's pray again before you try again!" I don't remember what I prayed but when I finished she said, "I'm not going to stick you again after that prayer" and with that she left the room. I wondered what I had said but knew I could trust the Holy Spirit for my good and His glory!

I wasn't sure what was going on but so far so good, at least I wasn't hooked up to that needle! Soon, the nurse was back and another nurse was with her. This nurse walked all around looking for a vein, too. This was so obviously God because I normally have big veins that are quite obvious to see. But suddenly these guys were hiding and nowhere to be seen. I thought about Corey Tenboom and while she was in line at the concentration camp, no one saw her Bible. God had done this for her and would do it for me! The new nurse walked back to the old arm and settled on a vein that she said might work. One part of me thought, "It's finished! It's over! It's too late to speak up and say anything now!" To my surprise, I found myself sharing something that was strong on my mind in bottom of that 11th hour! Right before she stuck me with that needle, I found myself saying, "Would you please call the doctor and tell him all of the problems I've been going through? I have suffered enough and I do not need this." And then I found myself saying, "We're a threefold chord here, would you pray with me and agree, if I'm not to have this done that God would touch his heart and he would say OK?" I didn't know how this new nurse felt about prayer but I didn't care at that moment. All I knew was I felt God leading me to speak up and I did. As I prayed, I felt the power and presence of the Lord and knew in my heart that something great was going to come from this. Within a minute or two one of the nurses came back, stuck her head in the door, and said, "He said 'forget it'"! Praise You, Jesus! He was healing me from my head to my toes and with the little things too! Deuteronomy 1:28-29 says, 'how can we go on, our scouts have demoralized us with their report; they say that the people of the land are taller and more powerful than we are, and that the walls of their towns rise high into the sky; they have even seen giants there but I said to you don't be afraid! (Verse 30) The Lord your God is going before you; He will fight for you!'

As I continued to get better, I was told that surgery seemed unlikely for now; however, surgery would probably be necessary in a few months. I would have to have part of my colon removed and the colostomy put in, at least temporarily. I thought about this and how my daddy had a colostomy before he died. I also knew that my dad was able to reverse his, but I still couldn't believe what I was hearing! As I lay in bed, I really believe in my heart that God spoke to me that I would not have to have the surgery. I felt that He had healed me and with eating the right things and avoiding the wrong things, I was going to be fine. That morning my friend Kathryn called me to share that she had had a vision the night before. She said that she saw me being sown up but she couldn't see the doctor's hands; God had healed me. It had happened supernaturally and this only confirmed God's word to me of what He had already done!

God showed me many things that day. "Don't wait! Don't worry! It's never too late! Pray! Speak up when you're to say something! And don't be afraid, for God is with you! When I walk through the valley of the shadow of death, I will fear no evil"!

Healing, Not Just For The Body

Matthew 4:23 says Jesus traveled preaching the good news even in the synagogues and he healed people who had every kind of sickness and disease. In Matthew 9:2 -7 Jesus healed a paralyzed man's spirit first and then healed him physically; 'Seeing their faith, Jesus said to the man "take heart son! Your sins are forgiven."' This man's body was in need of repair but the man's spiritual state was Jesus' first concern. Whenever I'm under what seems a deliberate attack from the enemy, I first ask the Lord to search my heart and show me if there is anything that needs to be removed in order for me to receive healing or deliverance. A lot of the healing I've received has been emotional and when God healed my emotions and my broken heart, healthy soil replaced a lot of dead dirt so I could be a fruit-bearing tree planted by streams of living water. He wants "yours truly" to be healed all over. He has provided healing for my spirit, emotions, and body! As I sought the Lord for healing, these were the scriptures I prayed:

> **"Lord, I believe that You forgive all of my sins no matter what I have done and that You will heal all of my diseases (Psalm 103:3). Lord, You have told me to speak to the winds and say this is what the sovereign Lord says, 'Come o breath from the four winds and breathe into these dead bodies so we can live again' (Ezekiel 37:9). Lord, breathe Your life into our marriage. Lord, I thank You that You heal every brokenhearted place in me and that You bind up all of my wounded places (Psalm 147:3). I know the plans that You have for me Lord. They are plans for my good and not for evil. They are plans for me to have a future and a hope (Jeremiah 29:11). When I am weak like I am right now, You carry me. It was my sorrows, Lord, that weighed You down. You were wounded and crushed for my sins and You were beaten so that I could have peace, and whipped so that I could be healed (Isaiah 53:4-5)."**

Scripture Used In This Chapter

James 5:14 Are any among you sick? They should call for the elders of the church and have them pray over them, anointing them with oil in the name of the Lord.

Psalm 147:3 He heals the brokenhearted, binding up their wounds.

Exodus 23:25 You must serve only the LORD your God. If you do, I will bless you with food and water, and I will keep you healthy.

James 5:16 Confess your sins to each other and pray for each other so that you may be healed. The earnest prayer of a righteous person has great power and wonderful results.

Psalm 31:14-16, 24 But I am trusting You, O LORD, saying, "You are my God!" My future is in Your hands. Rescue me from those who hunt me down relentlessly. Let Your favor shine on your servant. Save me in Your unfailing love. So be strong and take courage, all you who put your hope in the LORD!

Deuteronomy 1:28-30 How can we go on? Our scouts have demoralized us with their report. They say that the people of the land are taller and more powerful than we are, and that the walls of their towns rise high into the sky! They have even seen giants there--the descendants of Anak! But I said to you, `Don't be afraid! The LORD your God is going before you. He will fight for you, just as you saw him do in Egypt.

Psalm 103:3 He forgives all my sins and heals all my diseases.

Ezekiel 37:9 Then he said to me, "Speak to the winds and say: `this is what the Sovereign LORD says: Come, O breath, from the four winds! Breathe into these dead bodies so that they may live again.' "

Jeremiah 29:11 For I know the plans I have for you," says the LORD. They are plans for good, not for disaster, to give you a future & a hope.

Isaiah 53:4-5 Yet it was our weaknesses he carried; it was our sorrows that weighed him down. And we thought his troubles were a punishment from God for his own sins! But he was wounded and crushed for our sins. He was beaten that we might have peace. He was whipped, and we were healed!

MARRIAGE

You're Not His Mama, You're His Wife!

I had been reading a book by Stormie Omartian about praying for your children. I loved the prayers in her book and began praying them for my children. I soon began to pray these prayers for Arnold, too. I finally asked the Lord "Why am I doing this? Lord, would You bring to light any area in my life that's out of order and not right in my marriage?" The gentle voice of the sweet Holy Spirit put this thought on my heart, "because you treat him like he's your child"! The words "you're not his mama, you're his wife" struck sharp in my heart as God's arrow hit its mark. As the Holy Spirit brought me the truth I had prayed for, I was beginning to see that **blind spots** were called that for a reason and I wanted all the blinders removed from my eyes. With God's help, divorce court was not going to be an option for me! One day a friend shared the following: "Wanda, you've been at the front of the boat and you've been doing the paddling, but now your husband is going to come forward and you've got to remember, he's not going to paddle the boat the way you do."

What wise advice from my friend! Letting Arnold be who he was, flaws and all, was a hard thing for me to do. "Please show me, Lord, where I am treating my man like a child". God began to remove the blinders by showing me how I was acting and what I sounded like. "Why are you going that way?" "Why are you parking there?" "I tried to tell you!" "If you had just listened to me, this wouldn't have happened." The Lord began to speak to my heart truths that hurt but also help set me free. "Don't tell him what he needs to do, Wanda, just tell him what God has done for you." It seemed as if I was always the one getting the corrections from the Lord and needing to change. Why couldn't it be Arnold's turn? When would God be changing him? "Quit worrying about what Arnold is doing and let me handle him. I'll deal with him; you just deal with you" were the gentle words from the Lord.

Jezy Can Be A Woman Or A Man!

In the Old Testament, there is a story of Ahab, the king of Israel, and his wife, Jezebel (1 Kings). Jezebel was a very controlling woman and Ahab was afraid of her. I discovered that Jezebel, or the type of spirit she had, could be on a woman or a man! As I read and listened to some tapes about Jezebel, it dawned on me that Arnold and I both had some of her traits in us; a Jezebel spirit will manipulate others to see things the way he or she does. Jezebel was filled with the pride of self and wanting her own way. I read that this nature of Jezebel flourishes in an atmosphere of fear, insecurity, frustration, and confusion. Arnold and I were living in just about all of these. Jesus did not live this way! I began to repent of my behavior and the Jezebel traits I saw in myself. I prayed that the courageous spirit of Jehu would rise up in both Arnold and me (2 Kings 9:33). Jehu was the one who had the courage to slay old Jezy.

As I was praying for Arnold to become a Jehu, Arnold shared that God had given him a scripture and a promise. I was very excited about this but as time marched on I began to think that Arnold wasn't moving forward with what God had shown him to do. I really wanted him to jump on this and get going but he wasn't moving or changing fast enough. One morning I took every opportunity to share this scripture in a number of ways hoping to make it come off the page and work in my husband's life. I just knew I had scored a home run with all the different ways I had presented the truth from the Lord to Arnold. When I shut up, I found out that not only was God not impressed, Arnold was downright angry! I continued to seek the Lord on this because I so badly wanted God to move Arnold forward and make him more like Jehu. The Lord directed me to Isaiah 28:27 - 28. In this passage the Lord was talking about a farmer and said that the farmer doesn't thresh all his crops the same way. A heavy sledge is never used on dill; rather, it is beaten with a light stick. Bread grain is easily crushed so he doesn't keep on pounding it. The farmer threshes it under the wheels of a cart but he doesn't pulverize it. What the Lord was trying to teach me through His Word was that the farmer takes into account what each crop is like. Pounding truth into my man was not turning the grain into a loaf of bread; in fact, I had just pulverized the grain! As I prayed for more insight concerning this new truth, the Holy Spirit seemed to whisper the following: "Release Arnold from YOUR desire to see him climb higher on the corporate ladder; release him from YOUR desire to see him move forward from promotions; loose your husband from all YOUR expectations and desires!" I had to release Arnold; there was just no way around it -- that is if I wanted to follow God's plan with my life. I wanted to be delivered from any type of the old Jezy nature. God was showing me that I was to work in my own field and let Him deal with Arnold in His timing; I was to only be an ambassador for Christ (2 Corinthians 5:20). As someone once said, "an ambassador is not responsible for changing folks but to represent the king for whom he serves."

> **"Lord, I repent of trying to control and manipulate Arnold into changing into the type of man I thought he should be. Lord, help me to be your ambassador today in my own home where I keep longing to act the way I should. Help me not try to change anyone but 'yours truly'. Help me be your ambassador to Arnold, Lord."**

How We Talk About Someone Is Usually What We Think Of Them!

With that thought coming to mind, I came to realize that the way in which I spoke to my husband reflected a fairly low opinion of him. I began to resent Arnold because I felt he was trying to control me. And I didn't feel like he loved me and cared for me as he should. I did not speak these thoughts directly to him but they eked out in the tone of voice I sometimes used when speaking to him. God began to speak to my heart that 'A wise woman builds her house, but with her own hands the foolish one tears hers down' (Proverbs 14:1). Was I building my house, or was I tearing it down? What kind of materials had I been using? Was I speaking to my husband as one who had great honor and respect for him?

In Ephesians 5:33 it says 'Let the wife see that she respects and reverences her husband. That she notices him.' Well I noticed him all right but it was what he was doing wrong that I noticed most of the time. 'See that she esteems him and that she defers to him, praises him, and loves and admires him exceedingly.' After I read that I thought, "I will do all of that when he gets it together and treats me right". I found it strange that nowhere did it say, if my man treats me with respect, honor, and kindness then I will do these things. Normally, I love to follow the directions of the Lord; whenever He would speak to my heart to do something, I would take great pride in how fast I could do it. Whether it was to invite someone to my home, mail a tape, or make a bookmark, I would pride myself in being like Paul Young Cho when he said, "I pray and I obey"! Yep, that was me, except with this one thing: follow the plans and directions for my man! I had to pray that Love would be restored and Love would find a way before I could do that!

Get Out The Book And Pray, Wanda!

The thought came to mind to get out a book by Sylvia Gunter called "Prayer Portions". When I came across her prayers on praying for your husband, it reminded me of how God had touched my heart through her book a long time ago. I had gone downtown to have copies made of something that I do called "Pathmats". While I was waiting to pay, I noticed this pile of books in a box on the floor. I was drawn to them for some reason. When I said something about the books to the lady who was waiting on me, she said they were wonderful and wished she could give me a copy, but they belonged to another customer. When I got home, I didn't think anymore about the book but I noticed there was something stuck to the bottom of my box. It was a piece of paper that had a prayer for your husband on it and covered praying for his head and his mind. I liked it so much that I began to pray those things for Arnold and I wished I had the remaining pages so I could pray for the rest of his body parts. Much later, someone mentioned the book called "Prayer Portions" and I felt a tug on my heart from the Lord to buy a copy. To my surprise as I looked over the book, I recognized the same page that had been stuck to the bottom of my box and there were the other pages containing prayers to pray for my husband. Now my man would be complete!

Those changes I wanted to see in my man were not going to happen if all I was going to focus on were his faults. Those changes would come as the Lord first changed me, one prayer at a time. I had to let go of my resentment and expectations concerning Arnold. "If he would only change and do such and such" was going to have to go and be replaced by "Lord would You please change me?". I picked up another book about spiritual growth by Evelyn Christianson, called "Lord, Change Me"; she reiterated God's words to me. She said, "Lord, don't change my man. Don't change my child! Lord, just change me!" That touched my heart and once again, my focus was off my husband and back on myself. Little by little and over time, God began to put into motion the process of change.

God Had A Plan For Us, Too!

One morning the following words came to mind: "Prophecy, speak to the North, the South, the East, and the West and demand that they give back to you". At first, I was a little reluctant and questioned what I had just heard. But then I began to speak them out loud. I wanted to obey God with this, and by the next day, He had even given me a song to go with those words:

> "Prophecy to the North and South.
> Yes, prophecy to the East and West.
> Yes, prophecy --
> You've got to give back to me now;
> That is God's promise to me."

Matthew 5:8-9 says, 'Two things I request of You, Lord, First that I would be pure in heart and secondly, a peacemaker.' If I had these two things then there would be more fruit in our home than I could possibly find at the farmers market. "Cleanse my heart, Lord and make MY HEART PURE" was my cry. I wanted God to bring peace into our home, not perfection. Did Jesus ever belittle anyone? No, but I did! Did he walk in peace even when the devil was out there? YES, but I did not. Outside of rebuking a few good Pharisees in the church (like me!), Jesus treated everyone with kindness and compassion, regardless of who they were or what they had done. I wanted to be like that, too! I searched the Word for prayers that I could pray that would help obtain this new fruit. Deuteronomy 10:16 and Ephesians 4:32 were just two of those that I prayed often.

> **"Lord, only You can change my heart. Clean it, Lord and make it as white as snow. And would You help me in my marriage to be kind to Arnold. Would You give me a tender heart, and a forgiving heart. When I get haughty, would You remind me how many times You've forgiven me?"**

Mirror, Mirror, On the Wall – Who's the Fairest of Them All?!

Was I willing to eat some humble pie? I went to Florida with a friend and as we sat in the church waiting for the speaker to begin, the Lord spoke to my heart that he was about to place a spiritual mirror in front of a lot of folks in the church, "yours truly" being one of them. I had never thought about praying for a spiritual mirror. What did God show me in my spiritual mirror? I was beholding the problem and not the Lamb. I was beholding what was going on around me rather than looking to God and knowing that I could really trust Him. He would prove to me that in His timing He would work all things together for our good. The Holy Spirit was showing me that we all have flaws but we are all special. God began to show me that I could change no one except me. My mama had true wisdom when she said "every tub sits on its own bottom". What I had thought were the BIG SINS was just sin to the Lord; size didn't matter. Pride was at the top of His list and my opinion of my husband was one filled with pride! I remember reading something from Joyce Meyer that struck my heart and brought me to my knees. She said, "A person who has pride is judgmental and opinionated." Since I was both, the change had to occur in me.

I thought my advice and opinions were so good; I thought they would bring my husband into a better place with God. I thought a lot of things were right but now I was seeing that I, not Arnold, needed to be in a better place with God. I began to pray that I would truly see, with my spiritual eyes. God granted my request, spoke to my heart one morning, and directed me to Proverbs 27:15-16. 'A nagging wife is as annoying as the constant dripping on a rainy day. Trying to stop her complaining is like trying to stop the wind or hold onto something with greased hands.' Ouch, that kind of hurts! The footnotes in my Bible made it even clearer what God wanted me to truly see. "A quarrelsome, nagging, steady stream of UNWANTED ADVICE is a form of torture." In that light-bulb moment, I could finally see that I had been torturing my man. No wonder Arnold was trying to escape; he wanted to be free and get out of the prison I had put him in. The revelation from the Holy Spirit was rolling; He was now my sidekick and showing me many things. The footnotes continued: "When you are tempted to engage in this DESTRUCTIVE habit (repeating yourself, keeping on and on about something, arguing) stop and examine your motives. Are you more concerned about yourself (getting your way or being right) than the person you are pretending to help?" Oh, NO! A mortal wound!! There it was in black and white. God had just put another nail in my coffin – death of self! He sure was shining His light on my darkness. I so wanted to be right! I just had to get my point across to make sure Arnold heard me. This poor soul, my husband, was about to get a pardon. I was about to get my prayers answered and probably some of his, too! To die to self was what I wanted and what I prayed. I wanted to die to all self-centeredness and all pride. "Lord, show me anyplace where I am hindering my husband, rather than helping him". God definitely obliged!

God began to show me through a spiritual mirror that I had been pushing my family to change. I was trying to draw them closer to God by attending every possible church meeting, dragging them to every prophetic meeting I could get them to attend, and telling them about all the problems I saw in them. This was not working! They needed someone with a HUMBLE SPIRIT, not a religious one. They needed to see LOVE in me. They needed to see that they were acceptable to me and to the Lord. They needed to be convicted by the Holy Spirit, rather than me. They needed to see that we were still able to have fun and laugh, not always looking for everything to be a serious sermon from God. Jesus talked to people about many things, like farming and fishing. He found out what their interests were and went from there, without condemning them. My family needed to see that I loved them by listening to them and putting an importance on what they were interested in even if it was a ball game or a special board game they loved to play. They needed to see that I was willing to sit up late at night and just listen to whatever was on their hearts. My spiritual mirror reflected that this "religious boat" I was riding would not float. This inflatable, rubber boat was about to burst and sink, producing an "Ishmael" rather than the Isaac I so badly desired.

Go To The Bank And Make A Deposit?

"Go to the bank and make a deposit" was a thought that came to mind one morning. Thinking first that I didn't have any money in which to make a deposit, I prayed and asked the Lord what He meant by this. This was the thought that came to mind: "Deposit love, joy, and peace into your marriage, Wanda. These are all blessings from the Lord for your account." God wanted me to stop storing up riches here on earth and start storing them in heaven and one way to do that was by blessing my family. With deposits of love, joy, and peace into our account, these would work wonders where our marriage was concerned.

God says we are changed from glory to glory but it is a process. I was praying more than ever to be truly controlled by the Holy Spirit. 2 Timothy 2:23-24 says the following: 'Don't get involved with foolish arguments, Wanda, which only gets you upset and makes you angry. God's people must not be quarrelsome; they must be gentle, patient teachers of those who are wrong.' I wasn't to talk down to my man (or anyone else). I was not to treat him as if he didn't have good sense. I was to R E S P E C T my man but I hadn't quite mastered this lesson from God.

Arnold and I had gone with our son, Franklin, his wife and two very good friends to see a Giants football game played in Atlanta. On the way home, we stopped at one of our favorite places to eat and while we were waiting for our table, we looked around in their gift shop. Franklin called my attention to a sign on the wall and with a grin said "This one's for you mom"! The sign said the following. "The witch is back and she's casting spells"! Surely, he must have meant that for someone else. Surely, my beloved son didn't mean this one's for me! I've often heard "just ask your family to give their view point of you because they can see what others can't". They'll tell it like it really is. After I had a good laugh, I thought about what the sign said and got a message from our son's playfulness. Our words do cast spells. Our words can be healing and bring life and restoration or they can bring death by what they say and how they were said. If we are always putting another person down we're casting spells and if we're always putting ourselves down we're casting spells on us, as well.

When we are hurt by someone and feel rejected, it can be very hard to honor him or her. Someone once said that being loved is the most powerful motivation in the world. But our ability to love is often shaped by our experience of love. In other words, we can't give to someone out of an empty can. Being made aware of God's love for me was a fact I'd have to pray about, too. I didn't want to disobey God and not honor my husband like the Lord had asked me to, so I knew I'd have to pray. I would have to pray that I would die to self and follow what God wanted me to do. "Lord, help me to fall in love with You so I can love my husband, too". Romans 5:5 became my most frequent prayer. 'Holy Spirit come and shed abroad the love of God in my heart'. I knew if I was filled with the love of God that I could love everyone better, which included my man as well as me.

"Pray that God will show you ways to <u>bless</u> your man" was the thought that came to mind one morning. I wanted to hear the voice and direction of the Holy Spirit and asked Him to lead me in what I could do to bless Arnold. I was going to make a deposit in his "love bank"! Arnold had told me he'd be home for lunch that day and asked if I would have a sandwich ready for him. My first thought was a smart one, as in, "how come you can run a business and yet you can't make your own sandwich?" I decided to keep my mouth shut, THIS TIME. After all, I just asked my Heavenly Father what I could do to bless my man! And didn't the Lord say to do EVERYTHING as unto Him (Colossians 3:23)? That included speaking to my man as if he were the pastor or anyone else I honored and respected! I was learning too, that if I wanted my man to speak more respectfully to me, I was going to have to speak with more respect to him, too.

I began to prepare Arnold's lunch that fateful day, and decided that this time, I'd use a paper plate! The Christmas plate that I pulled out of the cabinet was a little premature in the season, as in about eight months before its time, but I decided that it would work quite well, especially since it had lots of compartments in it. I found all sorts of goodies in the fridge, to fill each little compartment, except for one small slot. I was kind of thinking aloud and said something to the affect of "Lord, what in the world could I put in here?" All of a sudden, the thought came to put a package of matches in there. "Matches", I wondered, "what could they possibly be for?" They would fit the slot, but that was about all, I reasoned. But I couldn't get the matches off my mind so, believe or not, I prayed! My prayer went something like this: "Lord, what could these matches be used for?" A simple thought came to mind: "Put a note with it and say, 'You can light my fire, ANY TIME!'" Arnold just loved it!

Again, I decided to make a deposit into Arnold's love account, just a little something that would bless him. So I prayed "Lord, would You bring something to mind that I could do to bless Arnold?" The words had no sooner left my heart and lips than my answer came. "Give him a flower!" Not flowers, but flower. Thinking it would be a little funny to give my man a flower, I thought about it and found myself voicing the words back to God again, "A Flower?" I reasoned that I had always heard of women being given flowers, but a man? And then I stopped and found myself saying, "NO MORE REASONING OUT EVERYTHING!!!!!" I Corinthians 1:25 says 'The foolish plans of God are far wiser than the wisest of human plans.' It was time for me to go forward with God and walk on the water and that meant I really had to trust Him.

A couple of days went by and I had forgotten about my man and his flower, until I went to the grocery store. I had already been in the store, waited in line, and brought my groceries out to the car when the thought came, "the rose"! I almost put it off one more time, "REASONING AGAIN!" This can wait; I've already been inside and stood in line one time; I can do this another day real soon! But I decided against this and went back inside, determined to find THE ROSE! I walked to the back of the store, even praying while I walked,

"Lord show me just the right one"! And there it was, a white rose. One single, white rose among roses of other colors was just waiting for "yours truly" to pick it up and take it home to my man. Without even thinking, I found myself taking things a step further, took the rose over to the lady in the flower shop, and asked her to put some baby's breath and a ribbon around it, too. I even smiled as I shared with her who was getting the rose! What was happening to me? Was this really God? All I knew was that I was glad I didn't procrastinate! And I was glad I had bought the rose! I was going to leave the store and run by Wal-Mart for a few minutes but with thoughts of this white beauty becoming an old faded glory, I decided to run by the house and leave the rose at home, along with a note for my man! When I got home, I suddenly remembered a little vase I had bought a couple of weeks before at the dollar store. I had listened to the still small voice, trying to be obedient and to die to reasoning. At the time, I didn't know why I bought it but now I knew its purpose. Taking the white ribbon from the green paper and placing it around the vase, I added a special note: *"I love you babe"*! With that, I left the rose standing there to greet my man when he came home for lunch and I continued with my errands! Arnold got home before me and saw his flower. He told me that he had never before received a rose and he was really blessed by it. I was blessed, too. I thanked the Lord for bringing the thought to make my man know that I cared and was thinking about him. "Love really does find a way"!

This Is The Fast I Am Calling You To, Wanda!

I had been to a Bible study one day where the teacher had taught about fasting (Isaiah 58) and I left there with one thought in mind: "What do You want me to fast from, Lord?" So often, my thoughts would go to denying myself of food in some way but the Spirit was bringing me truth, in this area as well. I was to fast from a bad behavior. God showed me he wanted me to fast "From Telling Your Husband What To Do"! I was not to tell my husband what needed fixing about him. I was to tell him what was right. I was not to tell my husband how I could have done something better than he could; I was to ask the Lord what I could do to be a better wife to him and what I could do to bless him. Refraining from telling my husband what to do and how to do it was a sacrifice. It was worse than *going without food!!*

God concluded my instructions with these powerful words, SERVE HIM SOUP, WANDA, NOT ADVICE! Yes, I was at the top of the list of those who needed to be changed. With the help of the Holy Spirit I began to fast as God directed me and in return was given this promise for new life in my marriage: Ezekiel 37:4&5 'O dry bones listen to the words of God. For the Lord God says see, I am going to make you live and breathe again. I will replace the flesh and muscles on you and cover you with skin. I will put breath into you and you shall live and know I am the Lord.' Dry bones, I realized was my dead marriage where love had long been gone and dried up like a parched and cracked riverbed. But the water would come as I sought the Lord for the scriptures He had for the restoration of my marriage and family.

"God, Your Word says that You will empower Your right hand and that You will crush the strength of mighty kings! It says You will open the gates of Babylon for us, too. And these gates will not be shut against us anymore. God, I know that You will go before us and You will level the mountains and smash down the gates of brass and iron. You have raised us up to fulfill Your purpose and not for a reward (Isaiah 45:1-2). We will neither hunger nor thirst. For You, Lord, will lead us beside the cool waters and You will make our mountains into level paths and our highways shall be raised above our valleys (Isaiah 49:10-11).

Lord, You are giving Arnold and me words of wisdom so that we will know what to say to those who are weary and even to each other. Morning by morning You waken us and open our understanding to Your will. Lord, help us to know what Your will is and die to our own will. Because You help us, Lord, we will not be dismayed! Therefore, Arnold and I have set our face like flint to do Your will and I know that we will triumph over our enemies (Isaiah 50:4, 7). You lift us out of the pit of despair, out of the mud and the mire and set our feet on solid ground and steady us as we walk along. You are giving us a new song to sing, a hymn of praise to You, God. And many will see what You have done for us and then they will put their trust in You too, Lord (Psalm 40:2-4).

Where is there another God like You, Lord? You can't stay angry with your people forever because You delight in showing Your mercy to Arnold and me. Help us, Lord, to give each other that same mercy and compassion and give it to others as well, even to those who offend us. Come, Holy Spirit, and work this in us (Micah 7:18). Put that kind of love in our hearts for one another. Above all else, Lord, help us to guard

our hearts because I know it will affect everything that we do (Proverbs 4:23). May Your peace and prosperity be all over the Reuben family (Daniel 4:1). And thank You, Lord, that You give our family victory in <u>every</u> battle!" (Psalm 18:43)

He's Praying With Me Now!

When I heard a friend share that he had bought the book, "The Power Of A Praying Husband" and was praying those prayers for his wife, I thought I would rapture. I had bought Stormie Omartian's book, "The Power Of A Praying Wife" and had been praying some of her prayers for my man for a long time. Surely, Arnold would want to pray those prayers for me now that he had heard this friend's testimony. But Arnold wasn't interested in what our friend was doing. And it did not go over very well whenever I would gently remind Arnold of how wonderful it was the way this friend prayed for his wife. I was still not going to get my husband to change, hard as I tried; here was another instance where "yours truly" was going to have to die to self. Once again, I began to let resentment grow because Arnold didn't seem interested in blessing me. Seeing I was about to go back around the mulberry bush again, I asked the Lord to deliver me from the desire to control and change my husband. I wanted to be content with Arnold, just like the Lord was.

A few months later, we made a family trip to the beach and while we were there, Arnold said he was going to go to Wal-Mart and buy himself a new book to read. Guess what he walked out of the store with? I can remember Arnold telling me to open up the blue Wal-Mart bag and there it was, "The Power of a Praying Husband"! And I didn't have to nag him to do it this time. This is not to say that I don't fall back into that trap of trying to talk him into something he doesn't want to do. Some of those old ways take a day or two to get rid of. But when I do see my true nature reflected in my spiritual mirror, I'm usually reminded very gently of another good word or two, from Zechariah 4:10. 'Do not despise the small beginning, Wanda, for the Lord rejoices to see the work begin and I want you to do that, too.' I want to be thankful for the little things. While we were at the beach, not only did Arnold start a new way to pray for "yours truly", he had a dream about me, too. The dream itself was a blessing from the Lord because Arnold hardly ever dreams. In the dream, God showed Arnold that I was like a teenager, having so much fun and that he had a young girl for his wife. Thank you, God, that I am now my husband's teenage wife! I felt like I was dreaming. It was absolutely wonderful to sit there beside Arnold while he went through the book searching until he found the one prayer he felt was just right for me each day. Then he took his time and began to ask me questions about all sorts of things that were coming to his mind as he read. He told me that he had never thought of praying for me some of the things mentioned in her book. God is blessing and restoring our home better than it was before. This blessing was like what God did for Job: 'And the Lord blessed Job at the end of his life more than at the beginning' (Job 42:12).

New Beginnings For Me And My Man

When I first started making out the list of scriptures to pray for my husband and our marriage, I began to write them out and before long, I realized they had taken on the shape of a Christmas tree. At first, I wondered why the Christmas tree and the prayers on it? Then I shared it with a friend and she said, "First, we have Thanksgiving, remembering all that we have to be thankful for. Then we have Christmas; God's blessing comes to us after we've thanked Him. Then we get New Years, new beginnings." Yes, we were getting many new, sweet beginnings.

Genesis 39:8
And the Lord
made all that Arnold
and Wanda did to prosper!
Psalms 1:3 Arnold and Wanda
are like trees, planted by the streams
of living water, bearing luscious fruit each
season without fail! Our leaves never wither
and all that we do shall prosper! Psalms 18:43
God gives Arnold and Wanda victory in every battle!
Psalms 18:48 God rescues our marriage from our enemies
and holds us safe out of the reach of their plans. Judges 3:9-10
Wanda cried out to the Lord and he gave her help and the Spirit
took hold of Wanda and the Lord helped her to conquer the enemy.
Psalms 18:3 All Wanda ever needs to do is cry out to the Lord.
O Praise the Lord – her marriage is saved from all of their enemies.
Psalms 33:8 Let everyone in all the land fear God and not man, and
let us be loosed by the power of the Spirit! The Lord is close to those
whose hearts are breaking.
And He rescues those
who are humbly sorry for
their sins! Jesus is the tree
of life! My thanks to all
of you who prayed!

Scripture Used In This Chapter

2 Kings 9:33 "Throw her down!" Jehu yelled. So they threw her out the window, and some of her blood spattered against the wall and on the horses. And Jehu trampled her body under his horses' hooves.

Isaiah 28:27-28 He doesn't thresh all his crops the same way. A heavy sledge is never used on dill; rather, it is beaten with a light stick. A threshing wheel is never rolled on cumin; instead, it is beaten softly with a flail. Bread grain is easily crushed, so he doesn't keep on pounding it. He threshes it under the wheels of a cart, but he doesn't pulverize it.

2 Corinthians 5:20 We are Christ's ambassadors, and God is using us to speak to you. We urge you, as though Christ himself were here pleading with you, "Be reconciled to God!"

Proverbs 14:1 A wise woman builds her house; a foolish woman tears hers down with her own hands.

Ephesians 5:33 So again I say, each man must love his wife as he loves himself, and the wife must respect her husband.

Matthew 5:8-9 God blesses those whose hearts are pure, for they will see God. God blesses those who work for peace, for they will be called the children of God.

Deuteronomy 10:16 Therefore, cleanse your sinful hearts and stop being stubborn.

Ephesians 4:32 Instead, be kind to each other, tenderhearted, forgiving one another, just as God through Christ has forgiven you.

Proverbs 27:15-16 A nagging wife is as annoying as the constant dripping on a rainy day. Trying to stop her complaints is like trying to stop the wind or hold something with greased hands.

2 Timothy 2:23-24 Again I say, don't get involved in foolish, ignorant arguments that only start fights. The Lord's servants must not quarrel but must be kind to everyone. They must be able to teach effectively and be patient with difficult people.

Romans 5:5 And this expectation will not disappoint us. For we know how dearly God loves us, because he has given us the Holy Spirit to fill our hearts with his love.

Colossians 3:23 Work hard and cheerfully at whatever you do, as though you were working for the Lord rather than for people.

1 Corinthians 1:25 This "foolish" plan of God is far wiser than the wisest of human plans, and God's weakness is far stronger than the greatest of human strength.

Ezekiel 37:4-5 Then he said to me, "Speak to these bones and say, `Dry bones, listen to the word of the LORD! This is what the Sovereign LORD says: Look! I am going to breathe into you and make you live again!

Isaiah 45 1-2 This is what the LORD says to Cyrus, his anointed one, whose right hand he will empower. Before him, mighty kings will be paralyzed with fear. Their fortress gates will be opened, never again to shut against him. This is what the LORD says: "I will go before you, Cyrus, and level the mountains. I will smash down gates of bronze and cut through bars of iron.

Isaiah 49:10-11 They will neither hunger nor thirst. The searing sun and scorching desert winds will not reach them anymore. For the LORD in his mercy will lead them beside cool waters. And I will make my mountains into level paths for them. The highways will be raised above the valleys.

Isaiah 50:4 & 7 The Sovereign LORD has given me his words of wisdom, so that I know what to say to all these weary ones. Morning by morning he wakens me and opens my understanding to his will. Because the Sovereign LORD helps me, I will not be dismayed. Therefore, I have set my face like a stone, determined to do his will. And I know that I will triumph.

Psalms 40:2-4 He lifted me out of the pit of despair, out of the mud and the mire. He set my feet on solid ground and steadied me as I walked along. He has given me a new song to sing, a hymn of praise to our God. Many will see what he has done and be astounded. They will put their trust in the LORD. Oh, the joys of those who trust the LORD, who have no confidence in the proud, or in those who worship idols.

Micah 7:18 Where is another God like You, who pardons the sins of the survivors among his people? You cannot stay angry with your people forever, because You delight in showing mercy.

Proverbs 4:23 Above all else, guard your heart, for it affects everything you do.

Daniel 4:1 King Nebuchadnezzar sent this message to the people of every race and nation and language throughout the world: "Peace and prosperity to you!

Psalm 18:43 You gave me victory over my accusers. You appointed me as the ruler over nations; people I don't even know now serve me.
Zechariah 4:10 Do not despise these small beginnings, for the LORD rejoices to see the work begin, to see the plumb line in Zerubbabel's hand. For these seven lamps represent the eyes of the LORD that search all around the world."

CHILDREN

Is That Your Final Answer?

On the TV quiz show "Who Wants To Be A Millionaire", the host, Regis Philban, would ask the question: "Is that your final answer?" The contestant could change his answer up to this point but once he indicated that it was his final answer then there was no going back. I didn't realize it at the time but this game was played frequently at our house as the kids grew up, with one exception. The kids would ask if Arnold and I wanted to change our minds about something in which we had already given an answer. Rather than standing firm, we typically gave in and changed our final answer. Somehow, Arnold and I had it backwards. Parents should obey their children and do what they want us to do rather than what we think is right for them! Surely, this behavior will gain us much respect from God and, of course, from them as well. I didn't want to deprive them or upset them and if Rebecca didn't get to go spend the night or Franklin wasn't allowed to continue with his game, I would have been doing just that. Talking the parents into things was a family tradition that carried on from my house when I was young, too. I would ask my mom for something and keep on asking until I got what I wanted. I didn't realize until I had children of my own that this was not a good thing. Manipulation was definitely not from God. Thank you, Lord that You can cut off a family trait if we pray, repent, and allow You to change us. By the power of the Holy Spirit, I began to break those generational curses that were all too familiar to our family! I asked God for boldness, courage, and love that wouldn't be afraid to stand up and say NO.

It Seemed To Me That I Made A Lot More Mistakes With Rebecca!

As children, Rebecca was very gentle and sensitive while Franklin was very "head-strong". My relationship with Rebecca was more challenging than the one with Franklin. This was due, in part, to the fear I had concerning Rebecca. I could see so much of myself in her. I didn't want her to be wild like I had been as a child; and therefore, I was not as loving or trusting as I should have been. My hardness on her did something to that very tender and sensitive heart but I didn't have the wisdom to see it at the time. Franklin, on the other hand, was strong-willed and needed more of the firmness that I was trying to dish out to Rebecca.

In my early years of motherhood, I was on a demon hunt. During part of my walk with God, everything I read concerned some form of demonic activity. My focus was on what the enemy was doing and on what other people said was evil. One fine day, I threw away my daughter's baby dolls because I had read somewhere that the names given to these particular dolls were evil, so out they went. No discussion - the babies were just trashed. When Rebecca came home from school that day, she discovered her babies had vanished. The baby bed that she and I had shopped all over for and finally found was now empty. I hadn't even thought about praying first to ask the Lord for wisdom and to show me His plan. I was so fixated in getting these evil spirits out of the house that I didn't even give much thought as to what my throwing the babies away had done to Rebecca. I thought I was protecting her until it finally dawned on me how sensitive she was and how much pain I caused her in the way I did this. I did the same thing to our son, too; I threw away all kinds of tapes and plastic men he collected. When I asked Franklin what his favorite childhood memory was, he said that he liked the family vacations that we took. And when I asked him what the worst one was, he said "when you got like you did and started throwing all my things away."

Decisions, Decisions, Decisions

As I look back over the mistakes I made along the way, I learned that our children can and do hear from God. This lesson taught me to listen to my daughter and to the still small voice of the Holy Spirit, not just to what man says. When Rebecca was in grammar school, her class went on a field trip to Washington. To some people it would have seemed like an awesome opportunity but Rebecca didn't want to go. Rebecca's class was told if anyone didn't go on the trip they would still have to go to school but drop back a grade and stay with a younger class during the time of the field trip. Even though being with the younger kids was demeaning, or un-cool to say the least, it was a small price to pay as far as Rebecca was concerned. I was agreeable with this because I had experienced homesickness when I was a child away at camp and it had left a painful imprint on my life. With this memory as a tormenting reminder, I decided that Rebecca shouldn't be forced to go on a trip that she didn't really want to go on. I told the teacher she didn't want to go and thought that would be the end of it. Later on, the principal called and assured me that Rebecca would regret it for the rest of her life if she didn't go and she'd be the only one in her class who didn't go on the field trip. Reluctantly, in the same way that I would let the kids talk me into something I wasn't feeling right about, I relinquished my parental rights concerning what I felt was right for my child and made her go.

Rebecca said it was the worst trip of her life and she was so homesick she couldn't stand it. She said she never wanted to leave home again. But with my continued rejection of her and my continued obsession of being at every prayer and Bible meeting, this child would soon change her mind. Rebecca learned who and what was more important to me by my actions, regardless of what my words said.

My Boat Was Sinking

As Rebecca was growing up, I didn't know I was losing her; it was a very slow and subtle process. She just didn't seem to want to be around me or the Lord because I had represented a God to her that would not have time for her and a God that had lots of rules and regulations and very little love and mercy. Mostly, I preached and preached about what she should and shouldn't do! Rebellion set in and I just couldn't figure out why. Arnold and I started attending a class on spiritual growth and a woman in the class shared how her mother's prayers had saved her children during lots of tough times. After class, I approached this woman to see if she would ask her mother to pray for Rebecca, too. She said she'd be glad to. About two weeks later, I ran into this woman again at a meeting. She seemed a little reluctant when she started sharing about her mother praying for Rebecca but she finally told me "My mom said to tell you that the Lord showed her that you were the one that needed to be changed first!"

I felt as if a rock had hit my forehead, just like when David killed Goliath with a single shot. I left the meeting a little confused, to say the least, and desperate to hear from God for myself. Had she been right? Was it me? The following morning, as I sat before the Lord, I asked Him to reveal to me if this woman was right. For once, I wanted to know the Lord's perspective. He answered "Yes" and that I was the one that needed to change first. God would continue to speak to me over the next twelve years or so and show me many ways that I needed to change.

Many times my first thought had been of Rebecca waiting for me to pick her up from school. But I wanted to stay and finish working on my project or continue praying or ministering. I had ignored the still, small voice of the Holy Spirit and paid more attention to man's desire for me. That zest and zeal to get all I could from the meetings, being responsible in the church's eyes, and trying to help everyone left my family falling short. I was hood winked by the enemy to think I was serving God when I didn't have time for my own kids. Jesus always had time for children and they loved to be around Him. He was filled with kindness and compassion – something I needed. God told David ten things that would bring him into His presence and one of those was the following: 'Those who come into my presence will be people who speak the truth from sincere hearts' (Psalm 15:1-2). That's what this woman did for me. She told me what I needed to hear rather than what I would have wanted her to say. The truth was spoken in love and it helped set me free. Proverbs 12:1 said 'To learn I must love discipline; it is stupid to hate correction'! I wanted to learn why my daughter did not want to be around me. I wanted to listen to what she was saying now and what she was interested in. Over time, I would learn a valuable lesson: telling someone I love them but never being there for them doesn't show them the love God talks about; it only shows rejection! I was also starting to see what my family had been trying to tell me for a long time. "You need balance, mom"! I would have to pray about that, too.

The Ice Cream Lady

As her mother, I thought I was the only one Rebecca would listen to. Unfortunately, she had heard all the preaching she needed from her mom about a God who destroyed things and who would point out all her wrong doings. How prideful of me to think that God was not capable of bringing someone else to get through to her! I began praying for the Lord to send someone that Rebecca would listen and respond to. I know God has different ways of doing things; He doesn't always use ice cream but this time He did. Before long, Rebecca's divine appointment walked into the ice cream store where she worked. When Rebecca came home that night, she was so excited. She told me about this remarkable woman, named Sherri, who had dropped by the store for an ice cream. This woman taught a Bible study at a nearby church; not only did Rebecca want to go to the Bible study, but she wanted to take me with her, too! Rebecca's new friend later told me that she had the strangest prompting to go by and get an ice cream on the day she met Rebecca. Sherri didn't know it at the time, but she was my answered prayer from the throne room of God. Sherri's many visits to get ice cream really blessed Rebecca. God does work in mysterious ways when He answers our prayers.

Several years down the road, God was still not through with this precious woman. Sherri had children, too, and one of them was a son named Randy Wilson. Randy and his wife, Denise, started visiting our church and soon became good friends of ours. Randy even designed the cover for this book! Talk about an ice cream cone going a long way; this one treated a multitude!

The Forgiving Parent

Several years ago at a church we used to go to, the pastor called all of the mothers forward for prayer. While we were being prayed for, all of a sudden, the pastor had a word from the Lord. He said, "There is someone here who has had a prodigal son or daughter. I don't know which one but you have made some mistakes and the devil has used these mistakes against you and is using you like a punching bag. Every time you start to get free, he reminds you of what you did. You're blaming yourself for all of their problems!" He went on to say he didn't know whom that word was for but I bet he knew before the prayer time was over. I couldn't stop sobbing. I knew it was a word meant for me.

One of the hardest things was forgiving me! I had let Satan rob me repeatedly by letting him read my scorecard over and over of what I had done to mess up the lives of my children my wrongdoings. I had to stop looking back like Lots wife did! These trips to the salt mines were killing me and those that I lived with! It was as if I was working in a prison, labor camp. I would go in, fill up my barrel with salt, and dump it, only to come back and load it up again, usually with the same barrel of salt. God spoke to me that day through my pastor and told me I was not to live in shame about my past mistakes; I was to forgive myself; I was to extend mercy and compassion to myself! Truth from the Holy Spirit was coming. He showed me that if I condemned myself then I would condemn others; if I loved and forgave myself then I would be able to love and forgive others. God gave me a scripture one morning and spoke to my heart through Isaiah 61:7-8: 'Instead of shame and dishonor, Wanda will inherit a double portion of prosperity and everlasting joy! For I, the Lord, love justice and I hate robbery and wrongdoing!' God was letting me know I'd been forgiven and He was giving me back **double for my trouble.**

After all the things "yours truly" was waking up to, God wanted me to be set free. I was going to have to stop looking back at my failures as a parent and forgive myself too! FORGIVE ME? Yes! My prayer went something like this:

> **"Lord, help me to forgive myself. Fill me with mercy towards others; fill me with mercy for myself. Come, Holy Spirit, and shed abroad the love of God in my heart. Lord, I'm sorry that I didn't listen to You when You gave me warnings of what I was supposed to do with Rebecca. Forgive me for getting so wrapped up in things I thought were serving You and praying for others more than for my own children. Show me, Lord, how to get my family back. Help me not to be like Lot's wife, always looking back and help me to see what I can do now to make a difference in the lives of my children."**

It's amazing what God will do when I start praying and repenting and asking the Lord to restore what the locust has eaten (Joel 2:25). A few years ago, Arnold and I were celebrating our 20th wedding anniversary. Rebecca called to wish us a happy anniversary and one thing led to another and the thought came to ask her how she felt when I threw away her dolls. She said "Mom I know they weren't real, but to me they were my babies. It would be like a mother walking into her room after being gone all day to find the baby bed and stroller empty. And all her children had been taken away and she didn't even get a chance to see them go or say good-bye." She went on to tell me the names of each one, which one had been her favorite, and the outfit she liked best. I had been so busy driving out evil, I hadn't even thought about how she must have felt or whether she had a favorite. They were gone and all I had felt was relief that the evil had finally been removed from our house. The only thing was, I was still there and I'm surprised that none of my family left! My "godly" actions drove my family further and further away from me and from the Lord! Unfortunately, my behavior had the opposite effect of the desire of my heart – for me and my house to serve the Lord. God began to teach me 2 Chronicles 7:14. I knew that if I would just humble myself, repent of my evil ways, and seek His face He'd heal my land. I wanted these things that had never been dealt with to come to light; apparently that's what God wanted, too, because that's what He was now doing, bringing darkness to light. Being able to talk about painful things of the past was a good thing!

God opened my understanding to see that just because I was ready to forgive myself, be a better mother, and spend quality time with her didn't necessarily mean that Rebecca was ready to receive this new mom in me. "Lord, change me" is a process; it would take a little more time and a lot more prayer.

She's In The Air Force Now!

When Rebecca grew into a young adult, she wanted to leave home so badly that she did something that surprised us all. She joined the Air Force. She checked herself out of college, enlisted in the Air Force and then came home to tell us what she had done. She was taking after her mom in a big way. No discussion, no input – just do it and don't tell anyone until after it's done. Our daughter would end up going to Texas, North Dakota, Florida, and Saudi Arabia. I began to pray and pray.

> "Lord, I thank you for giving Rebecca the strength she will need to perform the task (Isaiah 49:5). I thank you, Lord, that in Your mercy You will lead Rebecca beside the cool waters (Isaiah 49:10). I thank you, Lord that Your Holy Spirit will not leave Rebecca, for You have spoken (Isaiah 59:21). Lord, You knew Rebecca before she was even formed in my womb, before she was born. And You sanctified her and appointed her as being one of Your spokesmen to the world (Jeremiah 1:5). I pray she would get up and go out and tell whatever You tell her to. I pray she would not be afraid or else I know Your Word says You will make a fool of her. Lord, You have made Rebecca impervious to the attacks of her enemies! She is strong like a fortified city that cannot be captured, like an iron pillar and heavy gates of brass. Kings and officers will not be able to prevail against her. They will try, but they will fail! You are with Rebecca and You will deliver her (Jeremiah 1:17-19). Only if she returns to trusting You will You let Rebecca continue as being Your spokesman. Rebecca is to be an influence to them, not them influence her (Jeremiah 15:19). Help her, Holy Spirit, with the choices of her friends and remove anyone that would be a bad influence in her life."

I was blown away by this new wind that was coming into our home, but I also knew that wherever Rebecca was the Lord would use her and He would protect her. Rebecca would be gone for the first time in her life on Christmas and New Year's Eve, as well as her 21st birthday. She had been told that she would be able to call home and let us know she had gotten there all right, but this didn't happen. The only call she was allowed to make came on Christmas day and we weren't even there to receive her call. For the first time in years we were invited to someone else's home for Christmas and decided to go. It made me sick when I realized we had missed Rebecca's call. When I found out that she had waited in line for hours that day and had missed even eating in order to get that call through, it made matters even worse.

The Enemy Tried To Torment Me More And More

When we found out that Rebecca would be going to Saudi Arabia, I felt hot tears well up and a lump form in my throat. As the tears started to flow, all sorts of fears of what might happen to her started coming to mind. She could be raped! She could suffer from all sorts of wounds inflicted on her, and I was going to miss her so much I couldn't stand it! The Lord, in His mercy, led me beside those cool still waters to restore my soul that day when the thought came to mind to read in the book of Galatians. Had I ignored that still small voice I would not have received a blessing of inward strength from God! I didn't really know where to start in the book of Galatians other than at the beginning. I was determined that I was going to read until God showed me where I was supposed to stop. I didn't have to read very long before I found what God intended for my encouragement. Paul was speaking in Galatians 1:17 to me that day when he said: 'I didn't go to the apostles that were before me to find out what God wanted me to do. I went to the desert of "Arabia" to hear from the Lord'. Talk about exploding with joy! Fireworks were going off inside me at the excitement of what I can hear from God for my daughter, right in my own kitchen. My heart was racing as those words from Paul stuck in my heart. Our daughter was going to be in the same desert where Paul the Apostle had been. She was going to hear from God there, too, just like he did.

I also learned "don't get too comfortable; if the devil doesn't get you with his first shot, he'll send out another one, so buckle up". This second attack came when someone told me "the scorpions are terrible in Saudi!" God was on time with His Word again and rescued me with

Luke 10:19 'God will give Rebecca the power to tread upon the serpents and the **scorpions** and NOTHING WILL HARM HER, WANDA'! The Word got through to me.

As we heard of the impending danger of war, I knew there was a chance that Rebecca could be killed and I cried out to God as fear once again tried to take hold of me. "Lord, what can I pray that will help her now? There could be war at anytime and I can't be there." I wanted so badly to control this situation and go over there and be able to put a huge shield around her. Psalms 31 came to mind to pray for Rebecca that day as I sat quietly at the table with my Bible in hand. I prayed and spoke Psalms 31 aloud.

> **"Lord I trust in You alone. Don't let Rebecca's enemies defeat her and defeat me, too, through this fear. Rescue Rebecca because You are the God who always does what is right. Answer quickly when I cry to You; bend low and hear my whispered plea. Be for Rebecca a great Rock of safety from her foes. You are there with Rebecca and You are her fortress; honor Your name by leading Rebecca out of this peril, as well as those with her, too. Pull her from the trap her enemies have set for her. For You alone are strong enough. Into Your hand, I commit her spirit (Psalm 31:1-5). You have not handed her over to her enemy, but have given her open ground in which to maneuver (Psalm 31:8). I am going to trust You, Lord. You alone are Rebecca's God; her times are in Your hands. Rescue her from those who would hunt her down relentlessly. Let Your favor shine upon your servant Rebecca; save her just because You are so kind! But let the wicked be shamed by what they trust in; let them lie silently in their graves (Psalm 31:14-17). Blessed is the Lord, for He has shown me that His never-failing love protects Rebecca like the walls of a fort! (Psalm 31:21) Oh, love the Lord, Rebecca, and all of you who are His people; for the Lord protects those who are loyal to Him; but will harshly punish all who haughtily reject him . So cheer up! Take courage if you are depending on the Lord."(Psalm 31:23-24)**

We prayed. She stayed. And we all survived!

Small Beginnings Lead To Big Results

A friend had invited me to the beach for a little R & R. Going off for a weekend without my man was not something that I usually did but this time I felt the Lord wanted me to go. We needed it; after all, we were prayer warriors for the Lord and warriors do get weary. My friend and I had walked down onto the edge of the beach and put our chairs right there into the water. I figured there was no way JAWS was going to get me unless he could walk. As we sat there with our toes in the water, Rebecca was heavy on my heart. I had prayed so many times for our relationship to be restored but it didn't seem like it was going to happen. In fact, it seemed to get worse at times, with our gears stuck in reverse. As our chairs sank into the sand, Kathryn and I found ourselves praying for Rebecca. After quite a long time in prayer, the Lord began to show me that we were doing warfare right there on the beach for her. The enemy would be stopped through prayer, praise, repentance and believing God for restoration. I don't remember the exact words we prayed for Rebecca that day but when we finished, the thought came to drive over to the Air Force base where she was stationed and talk to her.

At the time, Rebecca wasn't even speaking to me, at least not more than a cordial hello when I would call her. She was mad at me for a lot of reasons. One of which was that I had told Rebecca how I felt concerning one of her boyfriends. I had told her that the young man had not passed my test and I felt he was Rebecca's Ishmael, not the Isaac I had been praying for her. Unfortunately, I did this in a critical, cut down sort of way. I'm sure this young man had some real good qualities but I didn't talk about any of those with Rebecca. So once more, a wall went up between us. It seemed that not only was I on her case about some of the girls she chose as friends but also about the boys she dated. If I had had a mama like me, I would have been mad at me, too. I was too quick to judge and speak what was on my mind and that was just one of my many downfalls where Rebecca was concerned. But I also knew that love could find a way and God was changing me first.

When I mentioned to Kathryn about driving over to see Rebecca she said that she would be glad to take me over there. With Kathryn, it was as if I had said "do you mind taking me over to Wal-Mart just down the street?" It was just one more way to bless someone. We prayed on the beach before we left asking the Lord if He would show us for sure that we were to go and that it was not just some impulsive idea of mine to run over there. As we both prayed, we sensed the Lord giving us a peace about doing this and decided to go forward with our plans. When we got to the front gate, we could go no further unless Rebecca gave us permission to come onto the base. When the guard called to let her know we were there, the response on his end wasn't very encouraging. His response went something like this, "Because your mom wants to see you!" I guess I had thought that with all the prayers we had prayed that day and the fact that we had driven all the way, there would be a great breakthrough. I wasn't expecting any balloons at the gate, especially since she didn't know I was coming. But her reaction left me with a double dose of hurt and disappointment.

After the man gave us the Ok to go in, we were told to meet Rebecca at a little gas station down the road. When we got there, Rebecca pulled up and I jumped out of the car and ran over to her. I was so happy to see her and I thought if she could just see me, maybe there would be a change. But Rebecca was as cold as could be. As she stood there in her uniform with her rifle in hand, she looked like a stranger. She was a police officer on duty and not my daughter that night. We talked for a few minutes about how things were going; I should say that I did most of the talking, which was not unusual. She spoke to Kathryn and then it was time to go; Rebecca had to get back to work. Talk about my bad experience at camp! It didn't compare with the hurt and pain I was having with my daughter now. As I started to get into the car, Rebecca called out to me and pulled something from her pocket. It was a bag of peanuts and a little bar of candy. She asked me if I'd like to have it, handed it to me, and then she took off. She was hurting and I was, too. I could tell by the pained expression on her face that she was not a happy camper, either, especially with me being there. As we drove away, I cried with my little packages in my hand. I looked back until I could no longer see her. I told Kathryn that it seemed like nothing we did that day made any difference. Nothing had happened like I thought it would.

Kathryn was ready with her shield to hold off the enemies' deadly, dart of lies and told me to look at something that did happen. "She gave you something, Wanda. Look at what she did do. It was a gift. Something she had that she wanted to share with you"! Yes, that was a move of restoration from the Lord and I hadn't even seen this small beginning. The Lord showed me He had started the ball rolling that night.

Kathryn shared a truth that turned on the light and exposed the lie from the enemy. I was reminded once again by the sweet, gentle voice of the Holy Spirit of a very special scripture. Zechariah 4:10 said 'Do not despise the small beginnings for the Lord rejoices to see the work begin'! When I looked up the footnote from my bible for this scripture, it made an even bigger impression on me. It said "God rejoices in what is right, not necessarily in what is BIG!" I would pray this scripture many times in the days to come and ask the Lord to let me see the small beginnings when they happen. I wanted a more thankful heart and needed that nudge from the Holy Spirit to remind me of all the little things in which I should be thankful. I was depending on the Lord now more than ever to restore what the locust had eaten. I knew that Job had received double for his trouble and I was hoping and praying that God would do the same for us, too. Again, I was reminded of 2 Chronicles 7:14 'when Wanda humbles herself. Prays! Seeks me! Turns from her evil ways, she gets her land healed!' This mother – daughter relationship was improving, if only a little at a time; it was a small beginning but I knew it would lead to bigger things.

The Neighbor's Dog

We had a precious little puppy that died several years back and we never did get another one. So I set out to adopt the neighbor's dog and he seemed more than willing to oblige me. Almost every day I would give him dog bones. At first, I would wait until I knew his parents would be at work to give him his special treats. Rather than sneak around, I decided to ask my neighbor if he would mind if I gave his puppy some treats. He said "not at all". So my little buddy got his biscuits and I had the delight of sharing with my furry friend.

One day I didn't see him, then another day and still no buddy. I began to wonder if the neighbors were keeping him in the basement and letting him out when I wasn't there. But that just wasn't the case. I never did see him again and never found out what happened. He was just gone. The morning I realized he was really gone caused a sadness that went all over me. Then Rebecca came to mind and the pain she must have felt when her babies had disappeared, too, without a word to any of them. I cried and I cried, not because the dog was gone, but because my heart could feel, for the first time, a little of the sadness and pain Rebecca had felt. I was also able to see that the prayers for more understanding, mercy, and love were being answered. My heart was softening and God was changing me.

I called Rebecca and told her about the neighbor's puppy and how, for first time, I could feel some of her hurt. I cried as I told her how sorry

I was, but this time for a different reason. I had apologized before but only because of being convicted of what I had done. This time my heart was filled with mercy and compassion for her. I hurt so badly for her that I literally groaned and wept over the phone at what I had done to her. I also thanked the Lord that I could feel a little of what she had felt that day so long ago. I had been praying for more mercy in my heart and now God was giving me an opportunity to feel what it was like to have more compassion. God was definitely doing a work in my life and He was using Rebecca to accomplish it. Rebecca so understood; she didn't try to heap guilt or condemnation on me. It's as if I could hear her just nodding in complete understanding over the phone. No wonder she was going to be used by the Lord in such a mighty way. She possessed all three qualities of leadership that God told Moses he would need: wisdom, understanding, and experience!

Slowly, but surely as I prayed to be more understanding, little flowers started to grow. I began to listen rather than try to tell her what or how to do things all the time. God would show me that we didn't have to be perfect and follow all the rules to get His brownie points. He uses whom He chooses, too. In a dream, God made this point loud and clear to me. In the dream, Rebecca was doing all sorts of things for the Lord and being used by Him in a mighty way. She was soaring past me and a lot of good things were happening as God used her. It was simply amazing! After all my years and years of trying to serve the Lord, my beautiful, young daughter was becoming a mighty vessel of God – almost overnight. She hadn't been serving the Lord that long and hadn't been involved in church. And to make it even worse, she WATCHED SOAP OPERAS! God has restored this garden of a relationship and new blooms sprout all the time. We laugh together and have things to talk about now. We enjoy cooking, walking, and even praying together. Rebecca is an awesome prayer warrior but feels somewhat shy when praying in front of others. Many times, we will share a laugh together as we start to pray for someone because I'll say "Let's pray – you start!"

We are so proud of the woman that Rebecca has become. My mom knew from the moment Rebecca was born that she was extra special! She has a wonderful way with older people; young people like her; people of all races like her. We are all drawn to that special something that God put in her. Rebecca is truly beautiful inside and out!

Prayer And Praise Defeats The Enemy

Franklin and I didn't seem to have the problems that Rebecca and I experienced. They were both so different, as with each gift from God. When Franklin was born, I was happy the whole time I carried him. The "Pampered Chef" had nothing on me! I had the pampered son. Rather than raising Franklin with a firm hand, I was always trying to please him. I wanted him to love and approve of me just like I wanted all the men who were special in my life to love and approve of me.

Loving Franklin in this way created a very spoiled and strong willed child. But God had a plan for this strong and determined young man. I never dreamed that Franklin would need lots of courage for the line of work he would eventually go into but then God really does know better than I do. As a kid, Franklin and his friend, David, would go off to the creek at night with their boots on and go snake hunting. I can't believe I had the sense, or lack of it, to actually let my son do that! But mama had to learn to let go in more than one way. This was also a way for the Lord to train Franklin to become FEARLESS for the job he would have in the future. Franklin is now slaying these serpents with the Word. What an awesome prayer warrior he is.

He also endured some rough places that I would have never known about had it not been for a word given while I was at church for a Bible study one day. The pastor that was speaking stopped all of a sudden in the middle of his teaching and said "Wanda, I don't usually do this but the Lord is urging me to stop and pray now for your son". The pastor went on to share that some of the boys he could see in this vision from God were bad news. Though I don't remember the specifics of it, I do remember we stopped and prayed. Franklin was in a private Christian school and I wondered what could possibly happen to him there? I was numb and dumbfounded, to say the least, with fear coming all over me. I wanted to immediately run to school and get him out as quickly as I could; I was afraid of what might happen to our son. As I stood there with everyone praying, I heard the words "praise Me". I couldn't believe it. Was this God asking me to praise Him when some terrible warning was just given from a pastor who never stopped and said anything like this? But God was a God who could protect and restore. From what I have read in the Bible, praise is a way God uses to defeat the enemy. I don't know what would have happened had we not prayed that day, as well as PRAISED that day, but I do know God took care of it. And He loved Franklin enough to give us a warning.

Where'd This Come From?

I don't know where the idea came from for Franklin to be a police officer. But surely, it must have come from God because it was not something that was on our family tree. The thing that continued to come to mind as Franklin came closer to his graduation from the academy was how proud my daddy would have been of him. Daddy loved the police officers and many of them had a special place in his heart. Daddy had a wrecker service and through many wrecks on the highways, he came to know and respect the officers involved. Daddy died before Franklin was grown but I'll bet God gave him a front row seat in heaven on Franklin's graduation day. I remember sitting in the seats of the auditorium and waiting as the men and women in blue came walking down the stairs. There were about fifty of them in all and they marched down both sides of us. As they marched toward the front, I felt warm tears in my eyes and a lump form in my throat as I thought of how my daddy would have felt had he been there. How proud he would have been of Franklin; he loved him so much!

Letting Go Can Take A Long Time

Even though Franklin was grown and not living at home, he was still attending the same church as we did. I wanted the children to go where we did but I also knew that I had to let that go, as well. A part of me still held on because of the fear I felt during most of their young lives. When it was time for church to start, I would find myself turning back, looking, and waiting for Franklin to walk in. And if he didn't or was late, I became very frustrated. I'd sit there and wonder "what if he doesn't see where we're sitting and doesn't get to sit with us?" Or "what if he doesn't come"? Or "what if something has happened to him?!" God opened my eyes to this obsession with my children and showed me that I was letting fear control our lives. He knocked down some of those strong walls in my life and cut the invisible umbilical chords that seemingly were still attached after all these years. I prayed as the sweet, Lord Jesus was letting me see things:

> **"Lord, I break off any ungodly soul ties that are between my children and me. Lord, if any apron strings exist that need to be broken, would You cut them in two by the power of Your Holy Spirit? I also repent of fear and worry and ask that You**

set me free to love and trust You, Lord, where my children are concerned. Lord, I believe that You are quite capable of opening doors and drawing my children to wherever they need to be with You. I pray, Lord, that they would hear Your voice for themselves and that I would be willing to let them both go! I ask You, Lord, to help me to be sensitive to Your voice and to know what I am to do for them and when I am to do it. Help me not to get in Your way but just to enjoy and have fun with my children! I also break off any intimidation with my children so I can speak and share what is truly on my heart without being afraid of hurting them or getting them upset! And would You give me the courage and the wisdom I need when I am to say 'NO'?"

Waiting for Isaac

In the book of Genesis, God spoke to Sarah and told her she would have a child. She couldn't believe it and laughed about it. Then she lied to God when she told him that she didn't laugh. Sarah became very anxious when no child came forth. So she took matters into her own hands and told her husband to sleep with her servant. The servant produced a child, Ishmael, but this child was not the one promised by God. They missed God and had Ishmael. I get an Ishmael when I get anxious and take matters into my own hands. Arnold and I didn't want an Ishmael for our son; we wanted him to receive his Isaac.

When we felt Franklin was going in the wrong direction, we would pray and ask the Lord to remove any Ishmaels from his life. We prayed that any ungodly soul ties that would keep him in bondage to someone that he didn't need to be with would be broken. We began to pray consistently that God would bring him only his Isaac! Some of those prayers took a long time in coming and we had to watch Franklin walk through many things we'd rather he didn't but through these mistakes, he would create his own testimony. Romans 8:25 was a promise to me from the Lord and I was taking it to the bank where my son was concerned. Romans 8:25 says, 'But if we look forward to something we don't have yet, we must wait patiently and confidently.' I was confident that God had someone for my son! I knew in the same way that God had been looking after Franklin during those snake trips with David that the Lord would look out for Franklin with his special woman, too. There were a few detours along the way but God could take care of those as well. Here are some of the prayers I prayed for Franklin:

> "I pray that Franklin would be taught of You, Lord, and that his prosperity in everyway (mentally physically and spiritually) would be great (Isaiah 54:13-17). I ask You to make him like a tree planted by the streams of living water and that he would bear much fruit for You, Lord! (Psalms 1:3) I ask that You would make him a great man of integrity, that he would speak with the power of Christ, that Your eye would be upon him, and that Franklin's eye would be single upon You, Lord. And that his whole body would be full of light! (2 Corinthians 2:17) I ask that Your light would fill his heart, house, car and everywhere that he goes (Luke 11:35). Lord, when Your four living beings flew forward, the wheels moved forward with them. When they flew up, the wheels went up too. When the living beings stopped, the wheels stopped. For the spirit was in the wheels and wherever the spirit went, the wheels and the living beings went there, too. Lord, I Pray that wherever Franklin goes that the Spirit would go before him and be with him as he was within those wheels (Ezekiel 4:19-21). I ask You, Lord, to protect Franklin from all evil -- evil situations, evil influences, and evil people that would try to come into his life."

Something Good Was On Its Way!

When God brought Jennifer Wilbanks into Franklin's life on March the 8th of 2000, I knew He had heard Franklin's prayers, as well as ours. I didn't want to appear to be too anxious so I waited until about their third date before I started calling her my daughter-in-law. What made things extra special was that not long before Franklin met Jennifer, he had asked me to come downtown and meet him at his favorite jewelry store. He showed me a special necklace he had found and said "mom, when I meet the right girl this is going to be hers". That very Christmas Franklin gave that necklace to Jennifer. Their first date was over Pizza and soon led to a discussion about the Lord and each of their families. We were told the conversation went something like this. From Jennifer, "you've got to meet my dad" followed by Franklin's "you've got to meet my mom!" Here we were two believing parents, praying for our kids' helpmates and that they would be Godly!!!

Their second date was fast and furious with Franklin coming over and wanting to know if we would cook steaks and have Jenny over. He was even willing to fork up the money for some good ones. When Jennifer walked through those doors, it was like Christmas. She was better than the food on the table. What a precious gift from God. The joyful spirit of the Lord was all over her and to top things off she had her Bible in her hands. I couldn't believe my eyes. By now, I was calling her my daughter in law and she was calling me mom! O how I hated that! Out of balance and so very religious with the home folks, the last thing I thought would happen would be for Franklin to marry a girl like me. My next thought was, "Lord, please don't let her turn Franklin off and come on too strong like I did with him." Fear almost took root in me; I began worrying that Jenny would run him off with her love for the Lord. But the Lord reminded me that Franklin now loved Him, too!

I finally realized how serious their relationship actually was by their fourth date with this one small sign from the Lord. I had a big card that I kept a picture of Franklin on, along with our Grand-dog, Fletcher. I had many special prayers on that card for our son; it was a very special treasure to me. One morning things changed and as I picked up my prayer card to start praying for him, the thought came to me to give the card to Jennifer. "What are You talking about Lord?!" were thoughts going through my mind. "Is this really Your voice? Give up my prayer card with Franklin and Fletcher on it? I'm his mama; who can pray for him better than I can?!" Still puzzled but only for a moment, I realized this was God's way of telling me that Jenny was the one He had sent for Franklin. As much as I would have liked to think that my prayers would be the most powerful ones for our son, God showed me there was nothing more powerful than a man's wife to reach up to the Lord and pray for him. This was another truth from the Lord that would touch my heart. Peace finally came to my heart as God showed me that Jenny would love Franklin, too, and would pray for Franklin, as much, if not more than I would. With all my heart, I wanted what was best for Franklin and that was Jennifer Wilbanks. It took all of four months for these two to get married and make this divine appointment official! My prayer for this precious couple is for God to use them in a mighty way and for the enemy to be squelched!

"God, please shoot Your arrows and scatter all of Franklin and Jenny's enemies. And let Your lightning flash and their enemies be greatly confused! (Psalm 18:14) Arm them, Lord, with Your strength for any battle they will face and subdue their enemies under Your feet. (Psalm 18:39) Some nations boast of their armies but I pray that Jenny and Franklin will

boast in You, Lord, and what You have done for them. Nations will fall but Jenny and Franklin will rise up in their marriage, home and work; they will stand firm wherever they are! (Psalm 20:7-8) I also ask that You would send Franklin and Jennifer help from Your sanctuary and strengthen them wherever they need it." (Psalm 20:2)

Those Lessons I Have Learned

My children were growing up to be some awesome adults. God has a special plan and a purpose for each of them that are more powerful than my parental blunders. I knew that the love that was coming from both of them expressed a quality that had my mom and dad all over them, too. I really and truly loved my children. In the beginning, I just didn't have that tender, mother's heart and I didn't know how to get one. That is until a friend had the courage to speak the truth in love and then I realized that I could ask my Father for a tender, mother's heart and that He would give me one. My mom used to tell me "You're so heavenly minded that you're no earthly good". This was true; I just had to see it for myself. Thank God for people who love me enough not to let me stay where I was. I was so caught up in saving the world that I almost lost everyone in my family. Proverbs 4:25 said something else to me too. 'Look straight ahead, Wanda, and fix your eyes on what LIES BEFORE YOU'. Well I couldn't very well do that if I was focused on what I had done or where I had missed it with my kids and was always looking back. I wasn't forgiving myself as God had told me I was supposed to. With that constant turning back, I let the enemy run into my camp and keep me from the river God wanted me to start flowing in. I had to forgive myself for not being stronger and doing what I felt was the right thing to do. I had to forgive myself for not having a tender, mother's heart and for not being sensitive to the things that were going on in their lives. I had to forgive myself for preaching about love more than showing it. I had to forgive myself for not being perfect.

Oh, Those Ruby Red Slippers

In the movie the Wizard of Oz, the red shoes that Dorothy Gail wore fit her perfectly. And what I came to find out is when I try to make someone wear a pair of shoes that do not fit, all I do is trip them up and cause them pain. Wearing shoes that don't fit is not my idea of comfort, either. And I don't wear them usually for more than a day or two and then they find a new home. This reminded me of what I had been trying to do with my family since I had been saved. What they needed was to be saved from me! It didn't mean that somewhere down this yellow brick road of life that they wouldn't fit into their own glass slippers. But that would take wisdom and that meant I had to stop trying to force them to wear shoes that don't fit them.

Scripture Used In This Chapter

Joel 2:25 The LORD says, "I will give you back what you lost to the stripping locusts, the cutting locusts, the swarming locusts, and the hopping locusts. It was I who sent this great destroying army against you.

Psalm 15:1-2 Who may worship in Your sanctuary, LORD? Who may enter Your presence on Your holy hill?
Those who lead blameless lives and do what is right, speaking the truth from sincere hearts.

Proverbs 12:1 To learn, you must love discipline; it is stupid to hate correction.

Isaiah 61:7-8 Instead of shame and dishonor, you will inherit a double portion of prosperity and everlasting joy.
For I, the LORD, love justice. I hate robbery and wrongdoing. I will faithfully reward my people for their suffering and make an everlasting covenant with them.

Isaiah 49:5 And now the LORD speaks--he who formed me in my mother's womb to be his servant, who commissioned me to bring his people of Israel back to him. The LORD has honored me, and my God has given me strength.

Isaiah 49:10 They will neither hunger nor thirst. The searing sun and scorching desert winds will not reach them anymore. For the LORD in his mercy will lead them beside cool waters.

Isaiah 59:21 And this is my covenant with them," says the LORD. "My Spirit will not leave them, and neither will these words I have given you. They will be on your lips and on the lips of your children and your children's children forever. I, the LORD, have spoken!

Jeremiah 1:5 "I knew you before I formed you in your mother's womb. Before you were born I set you apart and appointed you as my spokesman to the world."

Jeremiah 1:17-19 "Get up and get dressed. Go out, and tell them whatever I tell you to say. Do not be afraid of them, or I will make you look foolish in front of them. For see, today I have made you immune to their attacks. You are strong like a fortified city that cannot be captured, like an iron pillar or a bronze wall. None of the kings, officials, priests, or people of Judah will be able to stand against you. They will try, but they will fail. For I am with you, and I will take care of you. I, the LORD, have spoken!"

Jeremiah 15:19 The LORD replied, "If you return to me, I will restore you so you can continue to serve me. If you speak words that are worthy, you will be my spokesman. You are to influence them; do not let them influence you!

Galatians 1:17 nor did I go up to Jerusalem to consult with those who were apostles before I was. No, I went away into Arabia and later returned to the city of Damascus.

Luke 10:19 And I have given you authority over all the power of the enemy, and you can walk among snakes and scorpions and crush them. Nothing will injure you.

Psalm 31:1-5 O LORD, I have come to You for protection; don't let me be put to shame. Rescue me, for You always do what is right. Bend down and listen to me; rescue me quickly. Be for me a great rock of safety, a fortress where my enemies cannot reach me. You are my rock and my fortress. For the honor of Your name, lead me out of this peril. Pull me from the trap my enemies set for me, for I find protection in You alone. I entrust my spirit into Your hand. Rescue me, LORD, for You are a faithful God.

Psalm 31:8 You have not handed me over to my enemy but have set me in a safe place.

Psalm 31:14-17 But I am trusting You, O LORD, saying, "You are my God!" My future is in Your hands. Rescue me from those who hunt me down relentlessly. Let Your favor shine on your servant. In Your unfailing love, save me. Don't let me be disgraced, O LORD, for I call out to You for help. Let the wicked be disgraced; let them lie silent in the grave.

Psalm 31:21 Praise the LORD, for he has shown me his unfailing love. He kept me safe when my city was under attack.

Psalm 31:23-24 Love the LORD, all you faithful ones! For the LORD protects those who are loyal to him, but he harshly punishes all who are arrogant. So be strong and take courage, all you who put your hope in the LORD!

Zechariah 4:10 Do not despise these small beginnings, for the LORD rejoices to see the work begin, to see the plumb line in Zerubbabel's hand. For these seven lamps represent the eyes of the LORD that search all around the world.

2 Chronicles 7:14 Then if my people who are called by my name will humble themselves and pray and seek my face and turn from their wicked ways, I will hear from heaven and will forgive their sins and heal their land.

Romans 8:25 But if we look forward to something we don't have yet, we must wait patiently and confidently.

Isaiah 54:13-17 I will teach all your citizens, and their prosperity will be great. You will live under a government that is just and fair. Your enemies will stay far away; you will live in peace. Terror will not come near. If any nation comes to fight you, it will not be because I sent them to punish you. Your enemies will always be defeated because I am on your side. I have created the blacksmith who fans the coals beneath the forge and makes the weapons of destruction. And I have created the armies that destroy. But in that coming day, no weapon turned against you will succeed. And everyone who tells lies in court will be brought to justice. These benefits are enjoyed by the servants of the LORD; their vindication will come from me. I, the LORD, have spoken!

Psalms 1:3 They are like trees planted along the riverbank, bearing fruit each season without fail. Their leaves never wither, and in all they do, they prosper.

2 Corinthians 2:17 You see, we are not like those hucksters--and there are many of them--who preach just to make money. We preach God's message with sincerity and with Christ's authority. And we know that the God who sent us is watching us.

Luke 11:36 If you are filled with light, with no dark corners, then your whole life will be radiant, as though a floodlight is shining on you.

Ezekiel 1:19-21 When the four living beings moved, the wheels moved with them. When they flew upward, the wheels went up, too. The spirit of the four living beings was in the wheels. So wherever the spirit went, the wheels and the living beings went, too. [21]When the living beings moved, the wheels moved. When the living beings stopped, the wheels stopped. When the living beings flew into the air, the wheels rose up. For the spirit of the living beings was in the wheels.

Psalms 18:14 He shot his arrows and scattered his enemies; his lightning flashed, and they were greatly confused.

Psalms 18:39 You have armed me with strength for the battle; you have subdued my enemies under my feet.

Psalms 20:7-8 Some nations boast of their armies and weapons, but we boast in the LORD our God. Those nations will fall down and collapse, but we will rise up and stand firm.

Psalms 20:2 May He send you help from His sanctuary and strengthen you from Jerusalem.

Proverbs 4:25 Look straight ahead, and fix your eyes on what lies before you.

POWERFUL PRAYER CURRENTS

Hello ….. Uh, God?

When I first started to pray, my prayers were relatively simple and consisted mostly of wanting to help people and see their lives changed. I still want this to happen but what I have come to find out is that prayer means so much more. Prayer is being in the "chat room" with God, so to speak and chatting with God would help me get to know Him better. By having His thoughts come to my mind about something I had prayed about, I would see why the Word said His ways were not mine. By my worshiping Him and thinking of Him rather than my problems so much of the time, my prayer time with God was giving me a relationship with Him I never knew could exist. John Wesley made a statement that struck a chord in me when he said, "Give me one hundred preachers who fear nothing but sin and desire nothing but God and I care not a straw whether they be clergy men or laymen. Such alone will shake the gates of hell and set up the kingdom of God on earth. God does nothing but in answer to prayer!" I was beginning to see this was true. Things began to come to me as I prayed and trusted the Lord more. I wasn't even praying anymore just to get answers to things; I was praying to KNOW GOD! For as long as I can remember the prayers I prayed were trying to find out what God's will was for my life but as time went by even that would change as I began to pray that I would know Him more.

As I began to read God's Word, I realized how life giving it is; I prayed and asked God to take His Word and make it real to me and show me how to apply it to my daily life. His Word is for healing, deliverance, and, best of all, for getting to know Him. I wanted to know what God thought. I cared about Him and came to find out how very much He cared for me through the Word and prayer. I found out that I didn't have to be in a certain place to really get to know Him or be in some leadership position within the church in order for Him to hear me. The Word says 'Pray without ceasing' (1 Thessalonians 5:17). At first, my prayer time was just in the mornings but I soon began to pray all the time: in the yard, in the car, at the kitchen sink, etc. Many times my prayers would change when I would seek God and ask Him to tell me what was on His heart that I was to pray. Our pastor shared that rather than telling God about your problems, start telling your problems about God. That worked! I loved it! The Lord also showed me that His

Word was truly a powerful weapon in defeating Satan and his demons. It is God's arsenal for the destruction of the enemy. My prayer life has matured tremendously from where it began. It has been a process, one of learning, faith, trust, and deliverance: learning to listen to what God was saying to me through His Word; growing my faith to believe Him even when the "stone" hadn't moved yet; and realizing that deliverance was for me, not just everyone else around me.

I Had Become An Intercessor

Several years ago, we started going to a new church. On Wednesday nights, the pastor would call for the intercessors and those who needed prayer to come forward. I had never heard of an intercessor before. I remember watching a particular woman walk to the front of the church to pray for others on many a Wednesday night. I always wondered where this woman got the words to pray for them, as well as the courage to walk all the way to the front of the church. Robbie, who is now a great friend of mine, seemed to know exactly what to say. While she was praying for people, I would watch the expressions change on their faces. As she prayed some would begin to cry and some just seemed to have a different look on their face. Where did she learn how to pray like this? I had prayed silently for others many times and would pray aloud along with the entire congregation when everyone recited the same thing. However, as far as being led by the Holy Spirit and praying aloud for someone without knowing what I was going to say was an entirely new ballpark. All I know is that God was calling me and I wanted to go! One night as Pastor Henley walked by me, I got up the courage and asked him "how do you become an intercessor?" Pastor Henley told me that he would be doing a seminar in the next few weeks on intercession and thought I might find some help from this. I went and I really liked it but I was still afraid to pray out loud for others! Fear consumed me with most of what I did in life. What will I say when I get up there? What if I'm wrong in what I say? What will people think of me while I pray for them? God knew I had this fear and to help me out of this rut and to further my prayer education, He directed my steps to a new Sunday class. The teacher asked us to turn to the person on our right side and give them one prayer request for them to pray for us the whole week. My prayer request was different than it had ever been before. I turned to the person on my right and asked her if she would pray that I would be able to pray for others without being afraid. To think that someone would be praying for me about this for a whole week was wonderful. This woman must have been praying mightily because God began to show me that my fears were based on my ability and my self-focus, rather than trusting the Lord to do this through me. I was consumed with pride, rather than the truth that the Holy Spirit would lead me and give me the right words to say at the right time.

Matthew 10:19&20 came directly to me one day as God began His work to set me free. Matthew 10:19&20 said 'Wanda Reuben, when you are arrested don't worry about what to say in your defense, because you will be given the right words at the right time.' I wasn't in prison, or I should say any physical one, but my mind was trapped. But God began to show me where that fear was coming from and that He had something better to offer me. 2 Timothy 1:7 said 'God has not given you this spirit of fear, Wanda. He has given you power, love and a sound mind.' My worry over my limitations and my ability, or lack of it, had imprisoned me. So I began to pray about it! I prayed for courage. I prayed for boldness and I prayed to trust the Lord.

> **"Lord, I repent of being fearful and worried about what I'm going to say. I don't want to be focused on my ability or lack of it. I ask You, Holy Spirit, to come and bring to my mind the right words. God, I want Your thoughts of what to pray for someone. I ask that You would set me free from my self focus and that You would help me to be more concerned about the person in need rather than my fear of what to say. I ask that You deliver me from this pride of what people will think of me if I say the wrong thing. I ask You for courage and holy boldness and for the power that comes from the Holy Spirit. I ask to be fearless like Jehu was when he killed Jezebel. I want to walk on serpents and scorpions and all over the plans of the enemy. In Jesus' name, AMEN!"**

Godly M & Ms Melt in Your Heart not Your Hands

I had prayed many times to be able to pray for others in such a way that they would have changed lives. But in order for me to do that, there were changes that had to be made in me first. God brought to my attention an article by Joseph Garlington. In it, Mr. Garlington said it was in his moment of righteous disapproval that the Holy Spirit responded, "You cannot be an authentic intercessor if you count any man's sins against him." I had become an official judge and had my man and others already declared guilty and ready for the judgment seat of Wanda! How could I possibly believe I would be effective in praying for my husband, my family, and others when I was holding them in judgment, rather than mercy in my heart?! It won't work; God sees inside my heart. I have to give mercy and forgive others and myself so I can live! I was in need of this special gift from the Lord – mercy. Where, oh where, was my heart of mercy?

'By mercy, truth, and the fear of God, evil will flee.' I had read Proverbs 16:6 many times but never really saw what it said. I had marched, protested, carried my signs, and kept my "hard disk" filled with the memories of what had been done to me. There was no delete button on my computer; I just stored my offenses inside, on my hard drive (heart). The result of a lot of pride and a lack of mercy was that I remembered almost every offense someone had done to me or had done to someone that I loved. I walked in so much deception. Sometimes I believed that I was not important to God and then other times I believed I was too important to God, with no sins at all! God told me to offer kindness and to be understanding to others, rather than preach and point out what was wrong with them. Unless God opened the door and told me to share something, I was only to love them; He would do the rest. God wanted me to see truth: It's up to Him to make the changes; I was just to pray.

"Lord, I claim Your Word: By mercy, truth, and the fear of God, evil will flee (Proverbs 16:6). Lord, fill me with more compassion and mercy. Give me that kind, understanding, and merciful heart and help me to do things the way You want them done. Lord, bring truth to me; make any deception that is darkness come to light. Lord, help me to be humble and to honor You."

My heart was filled with hurts and God wanted it cleaned out and filled with trust. Jesus was full of good things and I wanted to be that way. His heart was filled with meekness. Being meek was not weak as some would think. In the dictionary, it says being meek is being soft, gentle, and humble. Meekness was wisdom. Jesus' meekness towards his enemies was unheard of. Matthew 5:44 says 'Father, forgive them for they know not what they do'. He had such a deep compassion for them, while my tendency was to try to set them straight. Many times, I lacked the mercy I needed because my heart had been hardened by the hurt. I needed to be healed and delivered before I could pray more effectively. Bitterness had set its roots like a cancer in me. It cut off the flow of life and the very things that I wanted to see happen. Unlike some cancer treatments that destroy other parts of your body, God's m & m treatment of Mercy and Meekness offers no ill side affects!

I Met A Man Who Prayed In The Parking Lot

My next adventure in my prayer walk led me to a person named Bill; he was unlike anyone I had ever met before or since. I can remember being invited to his Bible study and after the class was over, he would line people up across the front of the room, seemingly execution style. And just like that, the people in the line were ready to be prayed for by others who he would assign. This man actually knew who needed prayer. He didn't have to wait and ask who wanted it; he knew. I sat there hoping this man couldn't read my mind; I was terrified at the thought of being one of those who would be called up front. I remember watching a woman get up and leave once it came time for the prayer session part. I always wondered why but I shortly figured it out; I bet she didn't want her mind read, either!

Bill told us about some of his encounters with praying for people in the parking lot, of all places. Terror gripped me as I thought about ever having enough courage to do something like that. Bill took me on a much deeper walk with God and I ended up doing some parking lot praying myself. I learned what His Word had to say to me. For the first time in my life, I realized that there is a real enemy and that Ephesians 6:12 was not just a folk tale. Ephesians 6:12-13 says that 'our struggle is not against flesh and blood but against the rulers, against the authorities, against the powers of this dark world and against the spiritual forces of evil in the heavenly realms; therefore put on the whole armor of God.' The enemy tries to steal, kill, and destroy and the prayer I prayed as a child, "now I lay me down to sleep", was not enough to keep me safe. The enemy roams about like a roaring lion looking for someone to devour (1 Peter 5:8); the body of Christ is in a constant battle with the enemy and I, as a member of that body, need the armor for protection and for my defenses; God's armor is effective and powerful because it is His armor, not my own!

I listened to Bill many times, as he led us in prayer by asking God to search our hearts and to reveal anything that needed repenting. I learned that to keep God's armor intact and effective, I would have to repent on a continual basis to make sure I hadn't opened a door for the enemy. Bill led by example and taught me that I could pray aloud, stand against the enemy, and go into the promise land with victory. With God's help, the help of those around me, and through the power from the Holy Spirit, I could sense a difference. I learned to stand and put on the full armor of God just like I put on my clothes every day. For this and all that I learned from Bill French, I am forever grateful!

PUTTING ON THE ARMOR
Ephesians 6:12-17

1. I place on my head the happy **HELMET of SALVATION**! It is happy because I have the joy of knowing that I will spend eternity in heaven with my Father. I wear this helmet to protect my mind from negative patterns of thinking. I bind 'the mind of Christ' (1 Corinthians 2:16) to my own mind.

2. I place in my hand the **SWORD OF THE SPIRIT** so I might know the Word and fight the enemy with each lie he tries to tell me. It is my most effective tool – defensive and offensive; it feeds my soul and gives me strength to come against those demonic attacks.

3. I place the **SHIELD OF FAITH** in front of me to protect me from any attacks and fiery darts of the enemy! Oh, how Satan wants to destroy my faith and beat me up until I feel like I'm nothing. With this piece of God's armor, I have faith to believe He will move all of my mountains. "Lord, increase my faith in You, for I can do all things through Christ who strengthens me."

4. I place the **BREASTPLATE OF RIGHTEOUSNESS** over my heart for protection. Oh, how sensitive my heart is! While I may feel rejected or carry unforgiveness in my heart, Jesus can cleanse me through His righteousness! With a new, unwounded heart that is protected through His righteousness, I can go out into the world and be a more effective witness for Him. I know as I stand against the enemy that it is His righteousness, not mine, the enemy faces!

5. I put on the **BELT OF TRUTH** to guard my loins! Satan is the master of deceit but God's truth will protect me from his lies. I must know and speak truth to others and myself at all times. Lord, bring me more and more of Your truths!

6. I put on the **GOSPEL OF PEACE** to cover my feet as I walk through everyday life. Sometimes I may be in turmoil or feel anxious, not knowing what direction to take. I will put on these special shoes of peace and walk the straight and narrow path because I know how much God loves me, so much that His son, Jesus, died in my place. I will walk in peace, protection and with a purpose!

Standing In The Gap

Someone that I loved dearly was having a lot of problems. I had kept silent about it, just sharing it with Arnold at our prayer table. One night at our Bible study, I decided I didn't need to keep quiet about this any longer. When darkness is brought to light, the darkness loses its' power! I spoke up about the issue and all the women were in agreement that they should pray for me and the one on my heart. All the women gathered around me, some laying their hands on me, and one at a time began to pray for me and the person I felt so burdened for. It was so powerful. I wept as I felt the Holy Spirit touch my heart and knew that God was there to minister to the one we were praying for, as well as me. The next day I saw the person we had been praying for and something she said let me know that I had made the right decision to "stand in the gap" for her in prayer. By sharing the burden I felt for this person with the women in my Bible study, I was increasing the power of prayer for her by the sheer number of people praying.

Prayers By Others

I continued in my prayer walk with many other teachers who I've never even met. I keep four other books with me besides the Bible: "Prayer Portions", by Sylvia Gunter; "The Weapons of Our Warfare", by Kenneth Scott; "The Power of A Praying Wife" and "The Power of a Praying Parent", by Stormie Omartian. These books are full of Word-based prayers on many, many subjects. Many times when I am praying for my family or for someone else, one of these books will come to mind and I will begin to look at the different prayers from these people until I sense the Holy Spirit leading me to stop! I pray what the Lord has given them to pray because I feel that we are to reap from the fields of others. I also want to make sure that I have my own fields planted with plenty of rich dirt and fruit trees growing everywhere in our yard, too. Looking in the Word, reading it for myself, and asking the Holy Spirit to make it come alive for me has given me more things to pray than I could ever imagine.

Father Knows Best

When I've told someone I was going to pray about something before making my final decision about what I was going to do, I have been told that this is just a "cop out". But this was about as far from the truth as one could get where I was concerned. I had read the scripture many times when Jesus said He did what His Father wanted him to do and He wasn't out to please man. I want to look to God to get my plan rather than to man, too! I do seek the council of wise men and women but I also know that looking to man can be a trap! PRAY ABOUT SOMETHING FIRST! Even the way I prayed for someone would change after I started asking the Lord to show me what I should pray for him or her. Arnold and I had been praying together each day for someone who had asked us to pray for his healing. One morning before we began our prayer time, I asked Arnold what he thought about us asking the Lord what He wanted us to pray for this man. Seeing no results with the continual prayers for his healing, maybe there was something more important that he needed. Arnold was in agreement and after just a minute of praying and listening, we both got our answer. As I thought about what we needed to pray for this fellow a big smile came over my face. When Arnold asked me what my smile was about, I told him what had come to mind: "pray about his stubbornness". Arnold smiled, too; he shared that he had the same thought to come to his mind as well. So our prayers for this person began with the condition of his heart and ended with the condition of his health!

As I read some footnotes from my Bible about seeking the Lord in prayer, it gave me just one more reason for asking God to show me what I needed to pray, rather than just diving in with my own thoughts from my own mind. The footnotes from my Bible said the following: "Pride is thinking more highly of my own wisdom and desires than God's." I was finding out that when I pray what someone else wants me to or what is on my mind, I sometimes don't get at the root of things and if I feel that I have no need of God's direction then I have fallen into one more place of foolish pride! "Lord, what do You want me to pray" has been one of the most fruitful ways I have ever prayed!

Pray Out Loud?? There's Power In The Spoken Word!

A friend and I joined a group at church for prayer one morning. We went through the requests and then started to pray. We just sat there quietly with no one saying a word. After a few minutes, I finally managed to muster up the courage to ask my friend sitting next to me, "why aren't we saying something? Why aren't we praying out loud?"

She murmured something to the affect that there was indeed a lack of power and something should be done. Neither of us did anything except to go back to our silent prayers. A few more minutes passed. I couldn't stand it; I decided to speak to my friend sitting next to me on the other side. She, too, agreed but the difference was that she did something about it. She wasn't timid; she courageously walked to the front of the chapel and indicated we should come together, hold hands, and pray out loud. When she did that, something broke. The ice melted and the Holy Spirit began to move. The Lord's presence filled that chapel and the power from praying aloud and in a group became almost tangible!

I love to pray aloud now. One of the most effective ways for me to pray aloud with a group or for someone in need is actually over the phone! I used to think that I couldn't really reach God unless I was right there, physically in the prayer meeting, but I have come to realize that God has all the phone lines bugged! Talk about a direct line! I have seen mountains moved and many answers to prayers prayed over the phone lines. It still takes courage for me to pray aloud, whether it's in a meeting or on the phone with a few other prayer warriors. I now know why God was continually bringing to my mind to pray for courage. When I have it, I can take out the enemy! God spoke to Joshua and Caleb to go in and see what the land was like and to find out whether people living there were strong or weak. What I had seen in my land was a lot of weakness. These are some of the scriptures that have come to mind to pray concerning strength and courage. When spoken out loud, they're POWERFUL!

> **Psalms 119:95 - 98** Even though the wicked hide along the way to destroy our family we will quietly keep our minds on Your promises. Help us Lord to love Your Word. It will make us wiser than all of our enemies because they will be our constant guide.
>
> **Psalms 119:101** Help us to refuse to walk the path of evil and remain obedient to Your words.
>
> **Psalms 119:117** Thank you, Lord, for holding us safe above the heads of all of our enemies!
>
> **Isaiah 41:10** May we FEAR NOT, Lord, and know that You are on our side. May we not be dismayed knowing that You will strengthen us.

Psalms 44:3 We will not conquer by our own strength and skill but by Your power, God, and because You smile on us and give us favor.

Exodus 15:2 You, Lord, will be our strength, our song, and our deliverer.

Psalms 18:32& 34 God arms us with strength and has made our way safe. He prepares us for battle and strengthens us to draw the bronze bow.

Psalms 18:39, 41&42 You have armed us with strength for the battle and subdued our enemies under our feet. You ground them, Lord, as fine as dust carried away by the wind!

Isaiah 45:24 For Jehovah is all of our righteousness and our strength!

"**Lord, I repent of any fear in my life. I want to trust You and be filled with Your love. I know that Your love will cast out all of my fears and I ask You to come, Holy Spirit, and shed abroad that love of God in my heart (Romans 5:5). I want my confidence in You Lord. I do not want to behold my problem. I want to behold the Lord. Come Holy Spirit and help me. Give me the Holy boldness and courage that I need. Make me into a force that the enemy has to contend with. Make my heart strong for You, Lord, and my forehead like flint!**"

WARFARE PRAYERS

Authority

David said, 'Who is this uncircumcised Philistine that he should defy the Living God?' When I read 1 Samuel 17:26, I knew I wasn't talking to the enemy like this. Why couldn't I speak like that? Usually, the enemy was intimidating me and trying to get me to run. "Speak like you know what's going on, Wanda. Speak like you know what you're doing, Wanda." I needed that pep talk and the words of David's prayer let me know it was time for me to stand up and confront my Goliaths. I needed to take authority over oppression, fear, intimidation, and a few other things in my life and the lives of my family. Even as a little child, I knew about these bed bugs: Good night, sleep tight, and don't let the bedbugs bite! As an adult, I didn't want these things to stay in our home any longer. I prayed:

> **"I cover myself and my family with the blood of the Lamb and I know that the weapons of our warfare are not carnal but mighty through God to the pulling down of every stronghold. I cast down every high thing that has exalted itself in my life and is contrary to the perfect will of God. I break any word curse that has been spoken over my family today and I speak blessing in their place. I say we have life. We will live, not die, and tell of all the good things that God is doing for us. I declare and decree that God's Word shall not return to us void Psalms 112:4-8 says when darkness overtakes us that light will come bursting in. We will not be overcome by evil circumstances. Lord, Your word says IF it were possible, even the elect would be deceived. So if You said it, it is not open for discussion. We will not stay in this situation, we will overcome. We will walk in light and truth with the help of Your sweet, Holy Spirit! We will take our thought life captive and start thinking on what is good, right, pure, and Holy. AMEN."**

Protection

Psalms 91 is called the Soldiers' Psalms. During World War I, the soldiers of the 91st brigade daily recited the 91st Psalms every day. This brigade engaged in three of the war's bloodiest battles. Other units suffered up to 90% casualties, but the 91st didn't suffer a single combat-related death. Put on the <u>full armor of God every day and pray the Word of God!</u>

Psalm 91

He, who dwells in the shelter of the Most High, will rest in the shadow of the Almighty. I will say of the Lord, He is my refuge, and my fortress, my God in whom I will trust! He will save you from the fowler's snare and from the deadly pestilence. He will cover you with His feathers and under His wings you will find refuge! His faithfulness will be your shield and rampart.

You will not fear the terror of night, nor the arrow that flies by day. Nor the pestilence that stalks in the darkness. Nor the plague that destroys at midday! A thousand may fall at your side, ten thousand at your right hand, but it will not come near you. You will only observe with your eyes and see the punishment of the wicked.

If you make the Most High your dwelling even the Lord who is your refuge, then no harm will befall you. No disaster will come near your tent, for He will command His angels concerning you to guard you in all of your ways. They will lift you up in their hands so that you will not strike your foot against a stone. You will tread upon the lion and the cobra! You will trample the great lion and the serpent.

Because he loves me, says the Lord, I will rescue him. I will protect him, for he acknowledges my name. He will call upon me and I will answer him. I will be with him in trouble. I will deliver him and honor him with a long life and I will satisfy him and show him my salvation!

John 14:6 Jesus said: I am the way, the truth, and the life. No one comes to the Father, BUT THROUGH ME! (That is God's way of salvation, none other!)

Rescue

Psalms 31 Lord, I trust in You alone. Don't let my enemies defeat us. Rescue us because You are the God who always does what is right. Answer quickly when I cry to You; bend low and hear my whispered plea. Be for us a great Rock of safety from our foes. Yes, You are our Rock and our fortress; honor Your name by leading us out of this peril. Pull us from the trap our enemies have set for us. For You alone are strong enough. Into Your hand, I commit my spirit. You have not handed us over to our enemy, but have given us open ground in which to maneuver. I trust You, O Lord. You alone are our God; my times are in Your hands. Rescue us from those who hunt us down relentlessly. Let Your favor shine again upon your servant; save us just because You are so kind. Don't let us be disgraced. Let the wicked be shamed by what they trust in; let them lie silently in their graves. Blessed is the Lord for he has shown me that His never-failing love protects me like the walls of a fort. Oh, love the Lord all of you who are his people. For the Lord protects those who are loyal to him but harshly punishes all who haughtily reject him. So cheer up! Take courage if you are depending on the Lord.

Psalms 43:3 Oh, send out Your light, Lord, and Your truth and let them lead us.

Psalms 46:1 God, You are our refuge, a tested help in times of trouble

Isaiah 43:19 God, You are going to do a new thing; You have already begun. You will make a road through the wilderness for us and create rivers for us in the desert.

Isaiah 45:3 God, You will empower us with Your right hand and You shall crush the strength of mighty kings. God shall open the gates of Babylon. These gates shall not be shut against us anymore.

Isaiah 50:4 Because the Lord helps us, we will not be dismayed. Therefore, I have set my face like flint to do His will and I know that we will triumph!

Psalms 46:1, 2, 4, & 7 O God, You are truly our refuge and our tested help in times of trouble. So we need not fear, even if the world blows up and the mountains crumble into the sea.

Prayers For Our City

I had a strange dream one night. In the dream there was lava pouring down from the top of a hill. I watched it as it ran down the hill and slowly poured out over the city. There were people and animals that just walked right into it, completely oblivious as to what was happening. As it came closer toward Arnold and me, I wondered if it would destroy us. We quickly went into our house and climbed up on a ledge to escape the destruction. The lava came up to our house and shook the entire foundation but that was all. Then suddenly the lava was gone, as quickly as it had come.

The next morning I began to pray and asked the Lord what in the world this dream meant. What city would have lava in it? Why were we in it? The thought soon came that the city was Birmingham. There's no volcano in Birmingham! What did this mean? My next thought was of Vulcan. Vulcan is a statue that stands atop a mountain of iron ore overlooking over the city. Then I thought about what happens to iron ore when it melts. It turns into lava! This man of iron, Vulcan, had been standing over our city for years. Suddenly I made the correlation between the destructive lava and the destruction of many families in our city.

I began to do some research on our city and on Vulcan. In Greek mythology, Vulcan was the son of Zeus and was the god of fire and destruction. He was a powerful god who used flame as his weapon; he also had chains that were concealed on him. These chains would trap anyone that came close. Yes, the enemy had definitely bound our city with chains: chains of greed over how much money our city would make with the iron ore and chains of unforgiveness due to abuse, pride, and prejudice. Vulcan was also rejected by his mother, as the myth goes. What awful things to have looming over our city from his high perch! Whatever is on top does flow down. Rejection was running rampant, especially in families, and pride made many people think they were better than others, especially those of a different race. In my own home, I could see how much destruction had occurred from these terrible things. Pride had kept us from forgiving but humility would enable us to forgive.

I began to ask the Lord what I could do to make a difference. "How should I pray about this, Lord?" The thought came to mind to look up certain scriptures and speak them aloud. This was what Jesus did. He spoke the Word aloud and defeated Satan with it. I began to speak words of deliverance, too – in my prayer closet, riding in the car, everywhere I went. My God is definitely more powerful than the destructive force of the enemy. Our home has not been the same with these prayers of repentance and deliverance. Listed below are the scriptures for our city, as well as our family.

Exodus 15:15 The evil leaders in our city will be terrified and the evil nobles (those in high places) will tremble. The enemy and his plans will melt with fear and dread will overcome them.

Joshua 21:43-45 So the Lord gave us the land He had sworn to give their ancestors and the conquered it. And the Lord gave them rest on every side, just as He had solemnly promised. None of their enemies could stand against them, for the Lord helped them conquer all of their enemies. All of the good promises that the Lord had given them came true!

Judges 6:9 Lord, would You drive out our enemies and give us their land?

1 Samuel 10:18 God delivered us out of the hand of the enemy!

2 Samuel 22:2 Lord, You are our rock, our fortress, and our deliverer.

2 Samuel 22:18 You deliver us from our powerful enemies, from those who are too strong for us.
2 Samuel 22:29-30, 33 You are our light and You light up our darkness. In Your strength, we can crush an army. With You, God, we can scale a wall. You are our strong fortress and You have made our way safe.

1 Chronicles 4:10 O that You would bless us Lord, and extend our lands. Please be with us and our family in all that we do. And would You keep us from trouble and pain?

Job 36:15 You deliver the poor in their affliction.

Psalm 1 O, the joys of those who do not follow the advice of evil men, who do not sit around with sinners who mock at the things of God. Let our delight be in doing everything You want us to, Lord, and day and night think about Your law. Make us like trees planted by the streams of living water, bearing luscious fruit each season without fail. May our leaves never wither and in all we do, may we prosper. But this is not true of the wicked. They are like worthless chaff, scattered by the wind. They will be condemned at the time of judgment. For the Lord watches over the path of the godly, but the path of the wicked leads to destruction.

Psalm 9:3 Our enemies turn away in retreat. They are overthrown and destroyed before You, Lord. For You have judged in our favor.

Psalm 18:28 Lord, bring light to our lives, as well as to this city. Shine Your light brightly over Ensley, as well as the rest of the city.

Psalm 18:32, 34 Arm us with Your strength, Lord, so we can resist the enemy and say NO when we need to and go when we don't want to go. Strengthen us, Lord, to pull the bronze bow.

Psalm 32:7 God, would You release songs of deliverance over our city and over our home?

Psalm 34:7 For the Angel of the Lord guards and rescues all who reverence Him.

Psalm 59:1, 11 Rescue us from our enemies, Lord. Protect us, Father, from those who would destroy us. In Your unfailing love, look down and help us. Stagger our enemies with Your power, Lord, and bring them to their knees.

Psalm 69:36 The descendants of those who obey Him will inherit the land. And those who love Him will live there in safety.

> **"Lord, I pray that in all we do that we will obey You, no matter what You have asked us to do. Father, would You bring to mind anywhere we have not obeyed You?"**

Proverbs 16:6 By mercy, truth, and the fear of the Lord, evil will be atoned for in the city of Birmingham.

Isaiah 2:17 The arrogance in this city will be brought low. Pride will lie in the dust. The Lord Almighty will be exalted.

> **Lord, I renounce and repent of any pride in my life. God, would You search my heart and show me if any pride is hiding in my heart? I want Your coat of humility on me.**

Isaiah 10:34 The mighty One will cut down the enemy, as an ax cuts down the forest trees in Lebanon, over the city of Birmingham and in our home.

Isaiah 11:2 May the Spirit of the Lord rest upon us, the spirit of wisdom and understanding, the spirit of council and might, the spirit of knowledge, and the spirit of the fear of the Lord.

Isaiah 12:2 God, You have come to rescue our family and we will trust in You.

> **"Lord, we need Your confidence to do this. We need a confident heart! Deliver us from our fearful ones."**

Isaiah 18:16 You reached down from heaven, Lord, and drew us out of the deep waters. You delivered us from our powerful enemies, from those who hated us and were too strong for us.

Isaiah 32:7 Let the smooth tricks of evil men be exposed, as well as the lies they use to oppress the poor.

Isaiah 33:3 The enemy runs at the sound of Your voice, Lord. When You stand up, the nations flee.

Isaiah 33:21 The Lord will be our mighty one. He will be like a wide river of protection that no enemy can cross.

Isaiah 33:23 Our enemy's sails hang loose with broken masts and useless tackle.

Isaiah 45:13 God will raise us up to fulfill his purpose and He will direct all of our paths. We will, with God's help, restore this city and free His captive people, and not for a reward.

Isaiah 47:4 Our redeemer whose name is the Lord Almighty is the Holy one of Israel.

Jeremiah 31:11 And the Lord will REDEEM our city from those who are too strong for us.

Ezekiel 37:9 Then the Lord said, Prophesy unto the wind, prophesy and say to the wind, thus saith the Lord God, "come from the four winds, O breath of life, and breathe upon those slain in our home and in this city that we might live".

Daniel 6:27 He delivers His people, preserving them from harm; He does great miracles in heaven and earth.

> "It is God who delivered Daniel from the lion's den and it will be God who delivers us!"

Matthew 4:17 I pray that people in our home and in our city would turn from our sins and follow You.

> "Deliver us from the lion's den and set the captives free. Send us angels now and make this city a stronghold of Holy angels. Begin to make examples of some from hell."

Matthew 5:38-44 You have heard that the law of Moses says, `If an eye is injured, injure the eye of the person who did it. If a tooth gets knocked out, knock out the tooth of the person who did it.' But I say, don't resist an evil person! If you are slapped on the right cheek, turn the other, too. If you are ordered to court and your shirt is taken from you, give your coat, too. If a soldier demands that you carry his gear for a mile, carry it two miles. Give to those who ask, and don't turn away from those who want to borrow. You have heard that the law of Moses says, `Love your neighbor' and hate your enemy. But I say, love your enemies! Pray for those who persecute you!

> "Lord, may we walk in love towards those who have wronged us. Give us humility so we can forgive. Lord, would You show us what it means to love our enemies and how to go about it? Thank you for giving us the mind of Christ so we can forgive as He forgives us. And I speak healing to those who have hurt us."

John 8:32 And we shall know the truth and the truth will set us free!

> "I bind our minds to the mind of Christ and loose our minds from every wrong pattern of thinking. Lord, help us to think like You do and see things the way You do, as well.

Romans 12:2 May God transform the way we think in this house, as well as in this city.

Prayers For The Storms

We have had several tornadoes in areas around our city. I used to just hold on tight and hope that nothing would happen to us. Basically, just worry a lot! But times have changed. I've learned that I can pray even about this. Now when I hear of a storm coming, I get out my prayer shawl, so to speak, and go to work. I always ask the Lord to show me what I am to pray. One of the special hints came as I heard a man on the TV speak some very profound words that have really influenced my life. And now when the storms come, I pray this along with a few other things.

I had heard Reinhart Bonnke when he spoke on a TV program one day. I also heard him pray. A huge storm was scheduled to hit the area where he was speaking and the host asked Mr. Bonnke if he would pray about it. His words have stayed with me. He said "Lord would You take the stinger out of the eye of the storm?" How great the Lord was to give that man the insight to pray this way! What happens when a bee or wasp loses their stinger? NOTHING!

Psalm 107:29-30 He hushes the storm to a calm and to a gentle whisper so that the waves of the sea are still. Then the men are glad because of the calm and He brings them to their desired haven.

Matthew 8:26 And Jesus said to them, 'Why are you timid and afraid, O you of little faith?' Then He got up and rebuked the winds and the sea, and there was a great and wonderful calm.

> "Lord, I thank You for removing the stinger out of the eye of the storm!"

And oh, those songs of deliverance!
Psalm 32:7 says 'God gives us songs of deliverance' and I will sing these songs unto You, Oh Lord, even in the midst of the storm!!